GANDHISM

GANDHISM
A Quest for New Civilization

by
Late Prof. Dashrath Singh

Edited By
Smt. Kumud Sinha

KALPAZ

Gandhism : A Quest for New Civilization

Rs. 625

ISBN: 978-81-7835-829-1

Published in 2011 in India by
Kalpaz Publications
C-30, Satyawati Nagar,
Delhi-110052
E-mail: kalpaz@hotmail.com
Phone : 9212729499

Laser Type Setting by: Rudra Computer Graphics, Delhi
Printed at : Chawla Offset Printers, Delhi

Dedicated To

My Next Generation
Agastya, Mrinalini, Pulastya, Minakshi, Sunil, Meenal,
Tapas and Pakhi

The Finest Tribute to Gandhi

"Generations to come will scarce believe that such a one as this ever in flesh and blood walked upon this earth."

Einstein.

"Truth is hard as adamant, and tender as a blossom."

M.K. Gandhi
My Experience with Truth:
p. 184

"Truth without humility would be an arrogant caricature...... He (a Truthful man) has need to be humble."

M.K. Gandhi,
Young India: June 25, 1925.

"I do not mind harsh Truth, but do object to spiced truth. Spicy language is as foreign to truth as hot chillies to a healthy stomach."

M.K. Gandhi,
Young India: Sept 17, 1925.

Contents

Foreword

This book is a product of love and learning, the love of a gifted wife for her deceased talented husband, and the learning of the departed scholar.

Can there be an alliance more powerful than one between love and learning?

The late Professor Dashrath Singh spent a lifetime teaching, researching and reflecting. The ideas of Gandhi were his central concern. His wife, Dr Kumud Sinha, has spent a lifetime as Dashrath Singh's dedicated partner. His concern became her concern, his learning her learning, his passion her passion..

The result is this remarkable study of Gandhi's ideas by the wife-and-husband team.

Here is a Gandhi for those who are cautious about what the heart teaches, a Gandhi for those who want to engage solely with the mind, a Gandhi for intellectuals. It is a professor's Gandhi.

It is both analytical and comprehensive. The sweep is large but the probe is careful. To present Gandhi's ideas, the authors use a fine nib on a broad canvas. The details are painstakingly drawn.

The context is not restricted to India, it is global. Its ten chapters cover what you would expect in a study of Gandhi's thinking – truth and nonviolence. But they also (very appropriately) cover "modern" themes such as peace education, conflict-resolution, value education and good governance. Gandhi's understanding of the environment is touched upon.

Among the chapters that left a mark on me was the one on Gandhi and Structural Violence. It offers an insightful and fresh view of Gandhi. I was similarly struck by the thoughtful assessment of Gandhi's contribution to Indian culture. Yes, and all know this, he understood and represented that culture and stood by it, while also understanding and learning from other cultures. In addition, this book argues, Gandhi enriched and added to Indian culture.

Equally impressive is the analysis of Gandhi's concept of Sarvodaya. Though Gandhi gave powerful new meanings to the age-old concepts of Satya and Ahimsa, these were, as Gandhi said again and again, not his original ideas. But, as this book argues, Sarvodaya – everyone's welfare — was Gandhi's original idea. The book examines Sarvodaya from different angles.

I welcome and commend this valuable work and salute the spirit behind it.

Rajmohan Gandhi,
Urbana, Illinois, USA,
August 22, 2010.

Preface

We are living in a world full of destitution and oppression, where there is no way of living a 'good life'.

Modern civilization is based on materialism and therefore, it has created civilizational crisis. As culture refers to the behavioral aspects and life-style of civilization, it has disintegrated man, society and the nature. For the natural growth of civilization, a balanced and harmonious relationship between the different aspects of culture is essential. Gandhiji experimented with truth for whole of his life, in order to understand such relationship.

Gandhi's outlook was creative in every sphere of life and wisdom. His principles are based on practice of the truth, nonviolence and celibacy. Gandhi's truth is a life-style leading towards moral and spiritual progress in life. He believed truth to be fundamental to every aspect of life.

He perceived the violence inherent in the social structures of the world society. The structural violence is the cause of oppression in relationships. With an earnest hope, Gandhi advocated that it is possible to overcome this violence with adoption of non-violent means to lead life. Violent systems must be abolished from the society so that woman or any week person may get rid of their wretched condition – as the souls and feelings of every creature are the same. Truth recognizes every creature in same manner.

Our educational systems and political systems are also based on principles and practice lashed with violence. Educational system lacks the power of character-building, for want of morality, religion and all round growth of personality. Politics is also dominating and problem posing. Gandhi's education system is laden with human values and politics is pure in end and means. Education is the means of realizing the values - the basic needs of the people. Politics is for general welfare and good governance.

Peace is a harmonious state of being. Therefore holistic peace, mental peace, social peace, cultural peace, world peace and ecological peace are need of a growing society.

In Gandhi's opinion everyone needs learning with training, learning with courage and training of no anger, tolerance and universal brotherhood.

Gandhiji reminded about concept of 'Sarvodaya', which must be the guiding force in a civilisation. 'Sarvodaya' means everybody should progress- 'welfare of all'. Sarvodaya is a concept deep rooted in Indian philosophy – based on the highest truth-a harmonious blending of all the noble thoughts of East and West.

Mahatma Gandhi provides an outlook in all the fields of Indian culture, to project living condition of a better life. He stressed on selfless-service of the people. Gandhi's spirituality is 'inner–voice' or 'soul-force'. He synthesized science and spirituality and gave a new direction to the people. He believed that purity of means and ends, moral consciousness, goodness in activity, fearlessness, untouchability, practice of non–violence in every sphere of life and in every structure of society, will lead human being to salvation. All these practices will bring a living situation in a society to live peacefully with progress and welfare of all.

Mahatma Gandhi, right from his childhood, was very much aware about right or wrong. He used to think over everything before practicing it in his life. Einstein said about Gandhi, "Generations to come will scarce believe that such a one as this ever in flesh and blood walked upon this earth".

Gandhi's approach of solving the problems was directly based on truth. Therefore, his thinking could find out the way of a 'good life'. Gandhi's 'Truth' was the result of his experimental life. "As my vision gets clearer, my view must grow clearer with daily practice". He believed that high thinking and simple living cannot be separated. Likewise one cannot separate truth with knowledge and bliss, from goodness and beauty.

According to him, truth is the 'inner voice' and one can know that truth with the help of his conscience. He said, "Truth is what the voice within tells you". "Hard as adamant and tender as blossom", the truth is a moral concept to Gandhi - a purifying concept that purifies individual as well as political, social, economical and other environmental characters. It is the ultimate reality that can explain everything of the universe. It is "voice of God", "voice of conscience", and "voice of truth".

This truth plays a vital role in building a character and individual character is the central point that can make a family, then a society, then a nation and then the world a good and beautiful abode of living.

Gandhi perceived all the problems with a keen eye. He wrote about truth, faith, fearlessness, nonviolence, satyagraha, non-possession, labour, trusteeship, politics, economics, freedom, religion, swadeshi, brotherhood, brahmacharya etc. and above all sarvodaya. He said, " I do want freedom, but I want all these for the soul".

Late Professor Sh. Dashrath Singh, a professor of Philosophy and Gandhian thought, was a real Gandhist. He studied Gandhi, thought Gandhi and lived Gandhi. He had profound faith in Gandhian Philosophy and believed that only Gandhian philosophy of life can make the world a better place of living. All the paths of his thinking turned towards Gandhism and with his utter intense belief he started writing the book "Gandhism- A Quest For New Civilization".

He had a passionate enthusiasm- "miles to go before I sleep" - but the milestone came earlier and he went to a deep sleep, not to awake again. The chapters and contents of this book will reflect his thoughts, which are based on deep analysis of Gandhian Philosophy and contemporary theories.

I hope that this book will not only satisfy the intellectual hunger of the readers, but shall also help all of us in shaping our life in best manner.

Dr. Kumud Sinha
W/O Late Prof. Dashrath Singh

Introduction

Human life is a divine blessing of God; therefore one must live it lovingly and peacefully. Unfortunately complicated human mind has become self-centered resulting in the bad attribute of selfishness. That is why attitude dominates over a man. This attitude and the other bad virtues like lust, anger, pride, intoxication, delusion etc. brought human being on a path, which does not recognize love and peace. Human being has become tyrannical and violent. Love, care and affection are substituted by dominance and exploitation. The weaker section is dominated by stronger, which has caused a state of peacelessness and restlessness in the human society. A cycle of dominator and dominated is continuing. There is no rescue because the egoism has prevailed upon individual and on the society. In this civilization, we lack a balanced and harmonious relationship with everyone-with mother, father, children, nature, ecology etc. Materialism dominates over conscience. The term 'Truth' is confined to books only and it does not find a place in our life. We are in earnest need of a new civilization, in which all being will live happily and peacefully.

Gandhi's ideas about society, politics, religion, truth, culture, love, peace, development etc are outcome of his experiments in life, which provide realistic solution to the present crisis being faced by our society.

This book presents a thorough study of Gandhian philosophy and contemporary philosophies. Prof. Singh has explained that how we can hope for a new civilization of humanity, which will be free of imbalance in human relations, ecology and notions of development. He finds possibility of existence of peace and harmony in the world by adoption of the Gandhian philosophy of life.

I present this book to this civilization with urge and hope that all of us will be able to stir our thought and to make introspection in order to realign values of our life and to establish a new civilization based on truth. I shall be failing in my duties towards my husband if I omit to acknowledge the important and unforgettable role played by some gentle men in giving actual shape to this book. My heartiest thanks to Pulastya Pramachala, who helped me in editing this book. It was really very delicate and herculean task for both of us. My elder son Agastya Arunachal supported us with his valuable inputs, which gave us the courage and confidence to complete this work. I also thank Kalpaz Publications , who agreed to publish this book with all enthusiasm. The moral support given by Mrinalini, Minakshi, Sunil and Meenal is priceless and I wish them a good life ahead. My grandchildren Tapas and Pakhi provide me the reason and strength to think for a new civilization and therefore they have bigger role to inspire me to complete this work. May God bless them with peaceful and happy life. Prof. Singh, though left us early, but his teachings and guidance still guide me. I am sure that his soul will rest in peace with peace coming on earth.

Dr. Kumud Sinha

1

Civilization and Culture

Human civilization is as old as the conscious efforts of human beings to live a happy life on this earth and beyond. Truth is perfect and its realization is partial. No civilization on this earth can claim themselves to be perfect. Human civilization is the history of gradual realization of truth emanated from the problem of promotion of life securities. The evolution of intellect and science in human beings made life easier and comfortable. But in the quest of pleasure and happiness, human mind also produced innumerable commodities which are superficial rather injurious to better life. They have made our life restless, burdensome and unhappy. The over consciousness about securities engaged human mind in the production of devastating weapons,thereby posing threat to the existence of this planet. We have learnt to soar in the sky but failed to live harmoniously on this earth. We know how to live decently in individual life but are ignorant of living better social and human life. Thus, the civilization, in which we are living, is inadequate, inhuman, unnatural to co-existence and welfare to all. It is lacking some truth very essential for human progress. We need a new civilization which must have its foundation on truth and non-violence, science and spirituality and the truth of the outward world as well as the truth of inner consciousness. Gandhism is a quest for new civilization based on truth and non-violence covering whole field of human life.

The Concept of Civilization

The term 'civilization', literally means, making of city and city life. The Hindi equivalent of 'civilization' is 'sabhyata', which literally means, 'The ways and manners of entering into sabha – the congregation of civilized persons or royal court'. The meanings of both 'civilization' and 'sabhyata' denote that the concept is used to refer to the manners of life of certain high class people. Most of the anthropologists, therefore, view civilization as "a special type of culture – namely, a complex or high culture."[1] "In their opinion civilization is the culture of people who live in cities".[2] By 'people', they mean people living together according to accepted customs, that is, of acting civilly[3].

However, within last two hundred years, the term has assumed a different and wider connotation. Now a days, it refers to "achievements in such aesthetic and intellectual pursuits as architecture, painting, literature, sculpture, music, philosophy and science and to the success which a people has in establishing control over its human and physical environment"[4]. A civilization, therefore, is judged on the basis of how a people produce aesthetic and intellectual works of high merit and provides physical and social security for its members. Sociologists believe that, "civilization is comprising the sum total of human 'means' and culture as constituting the collectivity of human ends"[5].

Material prosperity is the foundation of civilization. It flourished with the growth of commerce and industries. This led A.N. Whitehead to say that commerce is the beginning of civilization. All the facilities of commerce and industries are available in the cities and hence, city is regarded as corner and symbol of civilization. Muller writes :- "Although civilization has rested on the labour of the village world, its history is the history of Babylon, Jerusalem, Athens, Rome, Constantinople, Paris, London. The basic truth however, is that a city is a symbol of both the best and the worst in civilization and all the risk of its great presumptions"[6].

Civilization involves a value judgement which is not shared by all cultures[7]. Those cultures which are materially undeveloped and less consumptive are deemed to be uncivilized, backward and primitive and they are looked down upon by those who are supposed to be civilized. This also leads to the concept of class distinction and class conflicts between haves and have-nots. The society is ranked as civilized and uncivilized on the basis of their material achievements. "The greater the extent to which a people produces aesthetic and intellectual works of high merits and provides physical and social security for its members, the more civilized that people is; and conversely the less a people realizes either qualitatively or quantitatively any of these tenets of civilization, the less civilized it is"[8]. Mahatma Gandhi, presenting the essence of western civilization, remarked, "The word civilization means that people living in it make bodily welfare the object of life".[9]

In the west, the concept of civilization is distinguished from the concept of culture. Therefore, it is desirable to discuss the concept of culture and its relation with the concept of civilization.

The Concept of Culture

'Culture' is a very complicated term. The western anthropologists and behaviour scientists hold that culture is the behaviour pattern of a group or society. It is applicable to "all human behaviour"[10]. They believe, "a society refers to a group of people who have learned to work together, a culture refers to the distinctive ways of life of such a group of the people. It is culture, which binds people togather"[11]. Culture is that part of life, which is learned by people as the result of belonging to some particular group. This learned behaviour is shared with others. It is our social legacy as contrasted with our organic heredity[12]. Kroeber and Kluckohn defining culture write :- "Culture consists of patterns, explicit and implicit, of and for behaviour acquired and transmitted by symbols constituting the distinctive achievements of human groups including their embodiment in artifacts, the essential core of culture consists of traditional ideas and specially their attached values, culture system may on the one hand be considered as products of action, on the other a conditioning influences upon further action."[13] Taylor defines culture as "that complex whole which includes knowledge, belief, art, morals, law, custom and any other capabilities and habits acquired by man as a member of society."[14] It is true that culture is acquired behaviour, knowledge and capabilities of people. But it is not always expressed in outward conduct. It is something internal also. "Culture is not strictly speaking, the visible act, the speech or product of these things. It is a way of thinking, feeling, believing. It is knowledge stored up (in memories of men, in books and objects) for future use- patterns for doing certain things in certain ways, not the doing of them- what is important is that some men know how to make them while others set a value on them, are unhappy without them, direct their activities in relation to them or disregard them."[15] Explaining more vividly the inner aspect of culture, Pandit Jawahar Lal Nehru, in his inaugural address of Indian council of cultural relation, New Delhi on April 9, 1950, in a dialogical style said;-

"Does culture mean some inner growth in man? Of course it must. Does it mean the way he behaves with others ? Certainly it must. Does it mean the capacity to understand the other person? I suppose so. Does it mean the capacity to make yourself understood by the other person? I suppose so. It means all that."[16] To Nehru, "Culture is the widening of mind and of spirit."[17] There may be national culture and the culture of the age. "But there is something that is deeper than national culture and that is human culture."[18] In the beginning culture is quiet and silent. Later on it manifests in innumerable ways. Nehru said, "Culture first of all is not loud; it is quiet, it is restrained, it is tolerant. You may judge the culture of a person by his silence, by a gesture, by a phrase or more especially by his life generally."[19]

Culture is not a generic concept. It is selective and it consists in a good way of life. Presenting the Christian point of view, Joseph Pieper writes: - "Culture is the quintessence of all the natural goods of the world and of those gifts and qualities which, while belonging to man, lie beyond the immediate sphere of his needs and wants. All that is good in this sense, all men's gifts and faculties are not necessarily useful in a practical way; though there is no denying that they belong to a truly human life."[20] Culture in this sense is a sort of worship, which combines sacrifice and sacrament together and which grows in leisure, not in busy life.

The Hindi equivalent of 'culture' is 'sanskriti', which is derived from prefix 'sum', root 'kri' and suffix 'ktin'. When the word is composed from 'sum' and 'kri', it means 'ornament', 'beauty', *'sarament'*, 'refinement' etc. denoting both the inner and outer qualities of man and society. 'Sanskriti' therefore, refers to good conduct and life-style of human beings. Vinoba tries to explain the word 'Sanskriti' with the help of two words-*'Prakri'* and *'Vikriti'*. Our natural impulses are 'Prakriti' and when they are given wrong direction in life, they become *'Vikriti'* – perversion. But if they are refined, they become 'Sanskriti' or 'culture'. Voice in human beings is *'Prakri'* to make noise of it is 'Vikriti' and composing harmonious and soothing notes from it i.e. music is 'Sanskriti'.

In the opinion of Mahatma Gandhi, culture is the subject of mind, heart and soul. He said, "Culture of mind must be subservient to the heart."[21] "A nation's culture resides in the hearts and in the soul of its people."[22] It does not mean that he was a mystic. He equally emphasized on the behavioural aspect of culture. Advising the students he said, "Inner culture must be reflected in your speech, the way in which you treat visitors and guests, and behave towards one another and your teachers and elders."[23] "Mutual courtesy and respect is the foundation of culture."[24] Gandhi believed that culture is the foundation-*the primary thing*. It must reflect in the smallest detail of conduct and personal behaviour like how we sit, walk and dress etc.[25]

The main characteristics of the Gandhian concept of culture are as follows:-

1. The preservation of any culture does not require the contempt of the others, rather it requires the assimilation of the best of the other cultures.[26]

2. No culture can survive if it attempts to be exclusive, for cultures flourish by mutual interactions leading to a greater synthesis.[27]

3. *Soul, being the spring of culture*, Moksha or self-realization is its goal which cannot be realized without good character or being moral.[28]

4. A good character needs the simplicity and spirituality in every walk of life.[29]

5. Realization of soul is not an isolated phenomenon. It is integral and hence needs all round development of human faculties-physical, intellectual, aesthetic and spiritual taken together.

6. Different cultures are steps towards perfection and therefore, no step can be claimed as destination. All cultures are imperfect and striving for their perfection. Hence, conflict of cultures is unnatural. In fact, there should be dialogue between cultures.

7. Truth and non-violence are two dominant qualities of soul and therefore, they must be applied in personal as well as socio-political behaviours.

8. A balanced culture must be structured on the principles of matter and spirituality. However, material science must work under the direction of spirituality.[30]

9. The ultimate reality is one and spiritual but its forms are many. It means reality is unity in diversity. This principle is also applicable in the matter of culture. All cultures have common goal to realize, but they have their own identities. In their distinctness, none is high or low. Culture contains both the elements of universality and particularity, tradition and modernity, and unity and difference.[31]

10. The progress of a culture lies in its ability of synthesis – synthesis of past with present, and the synthesis of one culture with another culture. However, the synthesis must not be rootless. It must be done in the frame-work of indigenous culture.[32]

11. The seed of culture lies in the soul but it manifests in the forms of different behaviours.[33]

Maharshi Aurobindo gives a more comprehensive and compact view on culture. He wrote: - "The culture of a people may be roughly described as the expression of a consciousness of life which formulates itself in three aspects. There is a side of thought, of ideal, of upward will and the soul's aspiration; there is a side of creative self-expression and appreciative aesthetics, intelligence and imagination; and there is a side of practical and outward formulation. A people's philosophy and higher thinking give us its 'minds' purest, largest and most general formulation of its consciousness of life and its dynamic view of existence. Its religion formulates the most intense form of its upward will and the soul's aspirations towards the fulfillment of its highest ideal and impulse; its arts, poetry, literature provide for us the creative expression and impression of its intuition imagination, vital turn and creative intelligence. Its society and politics provide in their forms an outward frame in which the more external life works out what it can of its inspiring ideal and of its special character and nature under the difficulties of the environment ...... none of them express the whole secret spirit behind, but they derive from it their main ideas and their cultural character."[34]

Thus, culture is manly consciousness of life in its different forms aspiring towards its highest goal and constitutes all the aspects of consciousness-cognitive, co native and affective.

Civilization and Culture

Civilization and culture, though closely related with each other, are different in their origins, effects on human beings and goals. The history of civilization shows that it grew with the development of science and technology with a view to solve the material and social problems of life. Agricultural civilization, industrial civilization and information technology civilization–all grew in search of better material life having both the good and bad effects on human beings, as science and technology lack moral consciousness. Cultures, on the other hand, have their origins in the belief, faith, customs, morality, religion and philosophies of different societies. Self realization is the goal of culture and for realizing this goal human beings sublimate their instincts and animal passions with the help of moral consciousness and religious feelings.

Civilization is external and concrete. It is visualized in our possessions. Cultures are basically ideal and hence end in themselves seeking perfection. The basic principles of civilization are utility, speed, enjoyment, accumulation and conflicts for self preservation. But culture, on the other hand, rests on the principles of sacrifice, self restraint, peace and self realization.

From the point of view of space and time, civilization is most wide. It covers up the global population and centuries of time. But cultures are many and they differ from society to society. They take relatively less time to change–Maurad Wahba rightly says that civilization is one and cultures are many.

The relation, between civilization and culture, is the relation of part and whole. We know that civilization is a type of culture found in the city life. But culture includes in itself all cultures of society. Civilization is also partial in the sense that it reflects only material aspect of life. Culture comprehends all the aspects of life – material, religious, moral, aesthetic and social. It consists in the whole style of living of a people.

Gandhi's Outlook on Modern Civilization

Mahatma Gandhi had great admiration for Christianity. He had also commendation for English people. He acknowledged indebtedness to the British culture. But his outlook towards European civilization was very critical. His criticism was not due to his superiority complex, but due to the compassion for those who were groaning under the heels of civilization. He also warned the Indians, who were charmed by it and trying to copy it in their life. Though, aware of his inability to give an adequate conception of civilization, Gandhi gave some descriptions of it in his **Hind Swaraj**.

To Gandhi, civilization is that which makes bodily welfare as the object of life. And therefore, all that facilitate towards this object are the symbols of civilization. Living in better built houses, wearing variety of dresses, use of revolver and guns for physical security, use of machinery for productive and non-productive works, printing press, railways and air-ships, telecommunication, delicately dished up food, sophisticated tools of luxuries, parliamentary system of democracy, legal system, allopathic treatment, heavy industries etc. are the emblem of civilization. Modern civilization attracts people to work in mines and factories and earn more even at the risk of life. It makes people slave by temptation of money and luxuries. In brief, all round materialism is the mark of modern civilization.

"Modern civilization, Gandhi said, "does not take note of religion and morality; rather it teaches immorality and irreligion in the name of morality".[35] This led him to endorse the view of Mohammad to call it a satanic civilization.[36]

He opined, "It is my firm opinion that Europe today represents not the spirit of God or Christianity, but the spirit of Satan. And the Satan's success are the greatest when he appears with the name of God on his lips".[37]

Gandhi argued that almost all religions of the world viz. Hinduism, Islam, Zoroastrianism, Christianity, Jainism, Buddhism and others teach us to remain passive about the worldly pursuits and active in the pursuit of God or divinity. They do not encourage our worldly ambitions, rather set a limit to them. "There was true wisdom in the sages of old having so regulated society as to limit the material conditions of the people".[38] But on the contrary the modern civilization arouses our worldly ambitions without any limit and takes no care of religion and morality. No doubt, in the name of religion, superstitions and malpractices flourish in society. But to Gandhi, "Humbugs in worldly matters are far worse than the humbugs in religion. The humbugs of civilization are not to be found in religion."[39]Civilization is like a mouse gnawing while it is soodthing us. When its full effect is realized, we shall see that religious superstition is harmless compared to that of modern civilization".[40]

Modern civilization, though materialistic, is unable to fulfill even the materialistic needs of all of the people. "It fails miserably in doing so."[41] In fact, materialism flourishes on the pauperism of the masses. To Gandhi, materialism and pursuit of wealth for the satisfaction of necessary wants— are two different things. Materialism may be understood as a belief that matter is the ultimate reality and the increase of material comforts for sensual satisfaction is the only goal of life. However, this belief is not desirable, for "self-indulgence leads to destruction and ruination to morality."[42] It "obviously can never be an ideal. There can be limit to the practice of an ideal. But unlimited self-indulgence, as every body would admit, can only result in certain destruction of the individual or the race concerned."[43] "Increase of material comforts does not in any way *conduce* to moral growth."[44] Gandhi condemned the material comforts but not the satisfaction of essential needs of the people. He said, "I do want growth, I do want self-determination, I do want freedom, but I want all these for the soul. I doubt if the steel *age an advance* upon the flint age... It is evolution of the soul to which the intellect and all our faculties have to be devoted."[45] What Gandhi wanted, was the welfare of all which is not possible in few rolling in luxuries and masses starving for food and cloth. Wealth is not enemy to the growth of soul but excess of possession of wealth do. Materialism, therefore, is neither desirable nor sustainable.

Gandhi charged modern civilization as being aim less and without any clear direction. "Civilizations have come and gone and in spite of all our *vaunted* progress, I am tempted to ask again and again to what purpose?"[46] Not Gandhi alone, but the others too asked the same question. Wallace, a contemporary of Darwin asked the same question. According to him "Fifty years of brilliant inventions and discoveries had not added one inch to moral height of man kind."[47] Radhakamal Mukherjee also remarked, "Modern scientism or positivism left civilization without a guide for its goals *and strivings*. The vacuum was filled up by mass passions, hatreds, aggressions and force of irrationality unleashing social indignity and humiliation, man on the *scale* never previously experienced in the entire history of civilization."[48] In spite of the directionlessness of the civilization, "people come under the scorching flames believing it to be all good." "They become irreligious and in reality derive little advantage from the world."[49] According to Gandhi, "Industry is the chief symbol of modern civilization."[50] But "it represents a great sin". It is industry, which impoverished India and is leading Europe towards ruination. Machinery, to Gandhi, "is like a snake-hole which may contain from one to a hundred snakes. Where there is machinery, there are large cities; and where there are large cities, there are tram-cars and railways and there only one sees electric light."[51] Large cities are not conditions for the promotion of good civilization. "The large cities are a snare and useless encumbrance and that people will not be happy in them. There will be gang of thieves and robbers, prostitution and vice flourishing in them and that poor man will be robbed by rich men."[52]

Gandhi is critical of machinery, because it cannot lead us nearer to our goal and secondly it promotes the life of speed. The life of speed is not only violent but it also deviates us from the main purpose of life...... Gandhi said, "I protest against the mad rush of today, and instead of blessing the means by which modern science has made this mad rush possible, that is railways, motors, telegraph, telephone, and even the coming flying machines. I say that they are diverting man's thoughts from the main purpose of life; bodily comfort stands before soul growth; man has no time today even to know himself; he prefers a news paper or sport or other things rather than to be left alone with himself for thought."[53] Further, he said, "the modern *crag* for variety, for flying through the air, for multiplicity of wants etc. have no fascination for me. They deaden the inner being in us. The giddy heights, which man's ingenuity is attempting, takes us away from our maker who is nearer to us than the nails are to the flesh which they cover."[54] Gandhi believed that the mad desire to destroy distance and time was not meant for some philanthropic purpose. It is done only for exploitation and satisfaction of animal instincts. He said, "I whole heartedly detest this mad desire to destroy distance and time, to increase animal appetites and go to the ends of the earth in search of their satisfaction."[55] He claimed that he was working for a civilization in which possession of car would be considered no merit and railways would find no place.[56] It would not be an unhappy event for him if the world become once more large as it used to be at one time.[57]

Industrial civilization is evil in the eyes of Mahatma Gandhi. But he is not averse to all the machines and industries. What he opposed, was industrialism itself which is not indispensable for permanent welfare of human race.[58] The good of human race does not require quick instruments for "good *travel's at a snails pace*", it takes a long time. Therefore, if human race has to progress towards the good, it must avoid shortcut way and hurry result.

Modern legal system, allopathic system and parliamentary democratic system are also subjects of Gandhian criticism. These are the instruments of modern civilization which promote immorality in society. The lawyers, Gandhi said, "as a rule advance quarrels instead of repressing them.... They take this profession to enrich them, not to help others in miseries".[59] The profession of lawyers is "exposed to temptation from which few are saved". The allopathic hospitals, to Gandhi, are institutions for propagating sin. Doctors take less care of bodies than to increase immorality. They kill thousands of animals in the practice of *vivisection*. They violate our religious instincts. They become doctors to obtain honours and riches, not for service. Gandhi remarked :- "We may pretend to be civilized, call religious prohibition a superstition and wantonly indulge in what we like. The fact remains that the doctors induce us to indulge, and the result is that we have become deprived of self-control and have become affiminate".[60] British parliamentary democracy, in view of Gandhi, is no democracy. It is "a clock to hide Fascism and Nazism". It is "like a barren woman", who can produce nothing and "a prostitute loyal to none."

Thus, modern civilization, to Gandhi, is "a civilization based on violence of blackest type, largely negation of the divine in man and which is rushing *head long to its own ruin*."[61] It has given, "matter a place, which by right belongs to spirit. It has therefore, put violence on the throne of triumph and held under bondage truth and innocence."[62] Like some others, he also regards modern civilization a disease, but curable.

The spirit behind Gandhi's criticism of modern civilization is that it is materialistic, exploitative and enemical to the progress of divinity and morality in human beings. It is responsible for horrible disparities in society and hence the uplift of the masses is impossible in this civilization. Without the all round development of the masses, humanity can never progress even an inch further. The elites, who are the protagonists of civilization, can no long enjoy their privileges. They will have to face the unavoidable wrath of nature as well as society. If they neglect the long term interest of humanity in the greed of short term gain and permanent happiness of self-satisfaction for the illusion of sensual pleasure, they cannot save themselves from the bad consequence of social revolt and natural calamities and the very civilization will prove itself suicidal.

Some Remarks on Modern Civilization

Not Gandhi alone, but some others have also questioned the relevance of modern civilization. The eminent historian Arnold Toynbee Questioned- "will mankind murder Mother earth or will he redeem her? He could murder her by misusing his increasing technological potency. Alternatively he could redeem her, by overcoming the suicidal, aggressive greed that in all living creatures, including man himself; has been the price of the great Mother's gift of life. This is the *enagmic question* which now confronts man".[63]

Depicting the pathetic condition of modern civilization, Shepard B. Clough writes :- "Tensions have developed among groups which consider themselves rivals for material betterment, as for example, between labor unions and employees or between the have - not and the have nations. Changes in living habits, particularly those which provide anonymity and freedom in family discipline, have resulted in antisocial conduct. In some extremely congested urban areas and in periods of great social upheavals, crime and other social disorganizations are tremendous. Extreme form of nationalism – a blind irrational and emotional attachment to one's nationality and a belief that the advancement of the nationality's place in the world, is the goal of human endeavour – is negative factor in human organization. This resulted in international friction and the disastrous world war"[64].

Herbert Muller opines :- "We should not be surprised to find that the highest manifestations of civilization have involved the deepest contradictions... . As the possession of privileged few- specially the priestly class, it consolidated the power of the upper classes, raising them still higher above the illiterate masses who were condemned to blind obedience and aristocratic monopoly was the cultivation of knowledge for decorative, honorific, esoteric or sacred purposes, rather than practical or productive ones...... Applied knowledge was not only degraded but divorced from the higher learnings; the useful was opposed to philosophical and spiritual...... Enormous extension of knowledge has meant not only a narrowing of consciousness for many specialists, but an impoverishment of consciousness for the many others, who have regarded its severely limited descriptions altogether the most successful instrument of human reason that has been the mainspring of western civilization"[65].

According to Daisaku Ikeda, "The greatest single failure of modern scientific civilization must be the development of nuclear weapons and the resultant threat of nuclear war. The second failure with its unbridled *michanical prowess*, is the increasing disparity between poverty and wealth, something clearly understood by Gandhi. In the global scale, it takes the form of the north-south development gap. The third failure is the global crisis of environmental destruction and finally there is the weakening and impoverishment of the human spirit itself, the loss of the human vitality and the concurrent moral and ethical crisis".[66]

The private secretary of mahatma Gandhi, Mr. Pyarelal observed :- "By absorption more and more in the outer world of senses, man has been able to gain mastery over the physical world. But in the process he has lost touch with the wells of intuitive knowledge within himself. His understanding of himself has not kept pace with his understanding of the outer world. His physics has not taught him how to regulate his own self. In the result the very power which he has gained over his physical environment today threatens to turn against him and overwhelm him. Society must find an answer to this double challenge of a moral force and a religion and morality that have lost their sanctions that stares it in the face or perish."[67]

Gerald Heard observed: "Our problem today is of search not of new ends or lofty goals, but for means, the power to use a force which does not frustrate itself; something that will restore to religion and morality the sanction they have lost. Can we find spiritual powers equal to our unbalanced physical powers, the finding of which is a matter of life and death for civilization?" ... "We have today a society which must capsize unless our psychic knowledge can equal our physics. ... By this advance in psychological power, we may at last achieve a non-violent sanction for all human relationships and new approach in our relationships with animal life and a new insight into the inanimate."[68]

Deterioration in the quality of human life in developed countries, is also a warning to modern civilization. According to H.P.R. 1991 prepared by the United Nations Development Programme, about 13% of people in U.S.A. are still poor. Higher income and wealth have not necessarily led to improvement in qualitative aspect of life, such as education. Adults with less than secondary education, constitute 78% of population in Spain, 72% in Italy, 57% in Belgium and 49% in France. The behaviour pattern of the youths of these nations are also alarming. According to a research conducted in U.S.A. in 1986, it is reported that 58% college male students favour "to force a woman into having sex." According to another report, "one in four women responds had an experience that met the American legal definition of rape. This is not the case of U.S.A. alone, but the other developed countries also suffer from such vices. The large scale sell of pornographic magazines in the developed countries is its proof. Naomi wolf in her book **The Beauty Myth,** has given in detail the pornography business in the west. According to her, British pornographic magazines sell two million copies a year earning five hundred million Ponds. Sweden earns 300-400 million Kronor a year, U.S.A. earns half a billion dollar a year from the sell of pornographic magazines and eighteen million men buy per month a total of 165 different pornographic magazines. Thus, the store of energy, which should have been transmuted into higher form of creativity, "in the case of modern man, this reserve is dissipated in aimless sexuality, not only through physical abuse but also through 'Psychic haemorrhage' helped by entertainment industry."[69] Dr. Grey Walter, therefore, warned that this 'psychic bleeding' of the modern man, induced by pornography, voyeurism, erotic art, obscene advertising etc. "is evolution in the reverse gear and fraught with the most far reaching consequences to the human race."[70]

Gandhi's outlook towards modern civilization, not only gets its confirmation by social scientists of today but also by the contemporary phenomena of world situation. Excessive reliance on outward forces and consumerism through science, technology, heavy industries, city life, governments as well as foreign help and the neglect of self-reliance, self-restraint, religion, morality and spirituality that is the development of inner man, has posed several problems before human-kind. Indiscriminate exploitation of the earth, environmental pollution, deforestation, global warming, green house effects *depletion* of bio-diversity and water resources and climatic uncertainty-taken together have caused ecological imbalances. The tendency of modern man to become rich in over night without doing work, has resulted in to various forms of violences like loot, murder, terrorism, hijacking, kidnapping for ransom, conflicts including war, toppling of governments of weaker nations prosperous in minerals, scams and corruption in mass scale, making human life unsecured and helpless. Growing unemployment, mutual distrusts, self- alienation, drug addiction and regional imbalances are very serious problems in global society. Cancer, T.B., AIDS, Diabetes and many other mental diseases are due to the environmental degradation and choosing wrong style of living by modern man. Modern science, though annihilated the global distances, it failed to make this world as a village or family. On the contrary, it converted it into a competitive market promoting lust, greed and profiteering. The market economy has become so stronger that not only it enslaved the rationality of producers and distributors but the rationality of social managers and media also. Consequently, women including men losing their personalities became like commodities – things to be valued in the market. The gulf of disparities between have and have-nots deepened, the thread of social integrity weakened and the purity of moral and religious commitments shattered.

Concept of True Civilization

After denouncing the concept of modern western civilization, Gandhi presented a blueprint of true civilization in his **Hind Swaraj or Indian Home Rule,** basically found in the ancient Indian culture. His 'true civilization' presents a contrary picture of modern western civilization.

The modern western civilization, as we know, is materialistic and hedonistic and hence, believes in possessing more and more goods of consumption to comfort our physical life. On the contrary, true civilization is idealistic and eudemonistic. It consists in limited possession and good conduct, which help human beings to elevate inner life- a source of real happiness. Defining true civilization, Gandhi said, "Civilization is that mode of conduct which points out to man the path of duty. Performance of duty and observance of morality are convertible terms. To observe morality is to attain mastery over our mind and our passions so doing we know ourselves."[71] As a matter of fact, pleasure through the satisfaction of senses is very transitory. Human mind is such, which is never to be satisfied by consuming things of sensual pleasure. Gandhi said, "The mind is a restless bird; the more it gets the more it wants and still remains unsatisfied. The more we indulge our passions, the more unbridled they become".[72] It means that riches are not the necessary condition of happiness. The rich may be unhappy and the poor happy. Therefore, it is foolishness to hanker after accumulating wealth to increase happiness.

Moreover, it is beyond the capacity of Nature to fulfil our unlimited needs. "Nature has enough to satisfy our need but not to satisfy our greed"- Gandhi said. So in true civilization, happiness is realized by changing our outlook towards life. According to Gandhi, "Happiness and health consisted in proper use of our hand and feet"[73] It is the denial of manual labour, which has caused corruption in mass scale and innumerable fatal diseases in our society.

The modern civilization flourished in the cities. It is said that civilization is the culture of urban people. However, the culture of cities is not desirable from the moral and environmental points of view. Cities thrive on the exploitation of the toiling people of the villages. There is weakening of the social bonds in cities, which causes various types of immoral acts like robbery, prostitution, gambling, pick pocketing etc. The living condition of the poor in cities are worst than the animals. There are smokes, noise pollution, water pollution and sanitary problems. Therefore, a true civilization resides in the villages. People in the villages live under strong social ties which prohibit them to indulge in immoral acts. They live on their bread labour and enjoy real happiness of life. They live a natural life and therefore, are not burdened with artificial problems, which are making so called civilized life troublesome and burdensome.

In modern civilization, doctors and lawyers behave like masters of the people. They are no longer servants of the needy. The medical and legal treatments are so costly that they are beyond the reach of the ordinary people. In true civilization, first of all, the people will be less diseased and there will be little quarrel in society. If there are patients and quarrels, doctors and lawyers will serve them as people's servant and hence justice would be fair and medical treatment cheaper.

Modern civilization is founded on science and technology and therefore, is irreligious and immoral. It is godless. It has no concern with the promotion of morality. The true civilization is grounded in deep spirituality and promotion of characters in human beings is its primary concern.

The history of modern civilization is the history of industrialism, colonialism, imperialism, exploitation, domination and wars, which indirectly is the civilization of making others slave. Even the champions of freedom and democracy are not consistent with their theory and practice and live like dominating boss in the world society. But the true civilization believes in real freedom of human beings on this earth. Real freedom makes people self-dependent, self-disciplined and self-governed having deep faith in non-violence. Gandhi said, "It is swaraj when we learn to rule ourselves".[74] Further, "The swaraj that I wish to picture is such that after we have once realized it, we shall endeavor to end of our life-time to persuade others to do likewise. But such swaraj has to be experienced by each one for himself".[75] In brief, the real freedom in true civilization, is realized through control over ones senses and passions. A really free man and free nation will try hard for securing freedom for the others in a true civilization.

No doubt, so long society exists, there will be wrong, conflicts and imperfection in it. The modern western civilization believes in solving these problems with the help of arms and physical force, i.e. violence. This force is applied due to belief in metaphysical difference. The proponents and the opponents are different and hence the opponents must be dealt with physical or violent force. Man struggle for the survival of his existence, as Charles Darwin held. The true civilization believes in oneness of all lives. All living beings are essentially one and there is no real conflict in them. Their survival rests on their love to each other. Gandhi said, "The fact that there are so many men still alive in the world shows that it is based not on the force of arms but on the force of truth or love... The greatest and most unimpeachable evidence of the success of this force is to be found in the fact that in spite of the wars of the world, it still lives on". [76] Further he argues, "Thousands indeed tens of thousands depend for their existence on a very active working of this force, little quarrels of millions of families in their daily lives disappear before the exercise of this force. Hundred of nations live in peace."[77] Therefore, the true civilization has firm belief in "sacrifice of self is infinitely superior to sacrifice of others"[78] and "Soul-force is superior to the force of arms."[79] The active form of this belief is called satyagraha- a unique technique of defence, conflict resolution and redressal of the wrongs and grievances. Thus, true civilization gives a moral alternative of war and other violence.

The true civilization presents a different system of education. In modern civilization, education means knowledge of letters. To teach students reading writing and arithmetics is called primary education. In the higher education, we learn different sciences. Such education is an instrument both to be used and abused. They have little to do with the real life.

The structure of education in modern civilization is so built that it only imparts superficial knowledge to the pupil. Gandhi remarked, "Whether you take elementary education or higher education, it is not required for the main thing. It does not make men of us; it does not enable us to do our duty."[80] He gives a very fine example to support his thesis. Suppose, "A peasant earns his bread honestly. He has the ordinary knowledge of the world. He knows fairly well how he should behave towards his parents, his wife, his children and his fellow villagers. He understands and observes the rules of morality. But he can not write his own name. What do you propose to do by giving him knowledge of letters? Will you add an inch to his happiness? Do you wish to make him discontented with his cottage or lot? And even if you want to do that, he will not need such an education."[81]

The education in true civilization would be based on the definition of education given by Professor Huxley. Huxley defined education as such, "That man I think has had a liberal education who has been so trained in youth that his body is the ready servant of his will and does with ease and pleasure all the work that as a mechanism it is capable of, whose intellect is a clear cold logic engine with all its parts of equal strength and in smooth working order... Whose mind is stored with knowledge of the fundamental truths of nature... Whose passions are trained to come to heel by a vigorous will, the servant of a tender conscience... who has learnt to hate all *vileness and* to respect others as himself. Such a one and no others, I conceive, has had a liberal education."[82] According to Gandhi, character-building must have the first place in primary education, because, "A building erected on that foundation will last."[83] All this does not mean that Knowledge of letters is of no use. Gandhi clarified, "All I have now shown is that we must not make of it a fetish. It is not our kamadhuk. In its place, it can be of use and it has its place when we have brought our senses under subjection and put our ethics on a firm foundation.

And then, if we feel inclined to receive that education, "we may make good use of it."[84] However, this education is not necessary. It has only ornamental value and therefore, in true civilization, this will not be made compulsory. In true civilization, there will never be the standardization of language. Education will be given primarily in regional and national languages. International language will be learnt only to enrich mother tongue.

Dynamics of Civilization

Modern civilization believes in Freudian 'principle of ambivalence', Marxian theory of 'inherent conflicts in the groups of society' and Darwinian principle of 'struggle for existence' and 'survival of the fittest.' Consequently, the dynamics of civilization is from violence to greater violence in all the fields of life. It progressed from the use of gun powder to atom bomb, from less consumption to more consumption, from open politics to concealed diplomacy, from harmonious relation to suspicious relation in society and from natural solution of problems to artificial solution. But contrary to it, the true civilization is founded on the dynamics of non-violence to greater non-violence, and love for the individuals to love for the whole world. It had progressed and will progress on the principle of sacrifice of individual for family, of family for the village, of the village for the districts and the sacrifice of the whole world for the cause of soul or self-realization. It believes in the philosophy of life 'to live for the cause of others', and in the art 'to live without.'

Gandhi believed in the unconscious working of law of love.[85] To him, "Human society is a ceaseless growth, an unfoldment in terms of spirituality."[86] In 1940 he wrote in **Harijan,** "If we turn our eyes to the time of which history has any record down to our own time, we shall find that man has been steadily progressing towards Ahimsa. Our remote ancestors were cannibals. Then came a time when they were fed up with cannibalism and they began to live on chase. Next came a stage when man was ashamed of leading a life of a wandering hunter. He therefore took to agriculture and depended principally on mother earth for his food. Thus from being a nomad he settled down to civilized stable life, founded villages and towns and from member of a family, he became member of a community and a nation. All these are signs of progressive Ahimsa and diminishing himsa."[87] Further he argues that all prophets of the world taught the lesson of 'truth, harmony, brotherhood, justice etc. – all attributes of Ahimsa.' "Man as animal is violent but as spirit is non-violent. The moment he awakes to the spirit within, he cannot remain violent," "Either he progresses towards Ahimsa or rushes to his doom."[88]

Last but not the least machinery is the symbol of modern civilization. In a true civilization, the attitude towards machinery will go radical change. Technology will have a human face. It will not make the masses unemployed, environment polluted and the earth depleted. It will not turn human beings into slave and will never be used as a means of exploitation. It will be friendly to human beings in saving labour and enhancing efficiency. It will be developed to promote small scale industries. However, the heavy machines will not be totally discarded. It will work under state control for the small tools and instruments.

From all this, he concludes, "If we believe that mankind has steadily progressed towards Ahimsa, it follows that it has to progress towards it still further."[89]

Earlier in 1931, he argued, "That life persists in the midst of destruction and therefore, there must be a higher law than that of destruction. Only under that law would a well ordered society be intelligible and life worth living."[90]

Thus, Gandhi's concept of true civilization is actually a new concept of civilization. Truth and non-violence are its foundation. Synthesis of science and spirituality is its technique and re-structuring of society for moral and spiritual uplift its goal. Gandhism, in fact, is a quest for this new civilization.

References

1. Kluckohn, Clyde; Culture And Behaviour, (New York; A Free Press Paper Back, the Mac Millan Company, 1962) p. 20.

2. Ibid, p. 20.

3. Clough, Shepard B; The Rise and fall of civilization, (New York and London; Columbia University Press, 1961, Paper Back edn, Foreword) p. 3.

4. Ibid, p. 3.

5. Kluckohn, Clyde (1962) p. 20.

6. Muller, Herbert S; The Uses of the Past, (New York; the Oxford University Press, 1957) p. 54.

7. Clough, Shepard B; (1961) p. 4.

8. Ibid, Foreword, p. 3.

9. Gandhi, M.K., Hind Swaraj, (Ahmedabad; Nava jivan Publishing House, 1994) ninth reprint, P. 32.

10. Kluckohn, Clide; (1962) p. 20.

11. Ibid, p. 26.

12. Ibid, p. 25.

13. Ibid, p. 73.

14. Taylor.

15. Kluckohn, Clide; (1962), p. 25.

16. Chatterjee, N.N; Nehru's Thoughts on National Topics, (New Delhi; Publication Division, Ministry of Information and Broadcasting, Govt. of India, 1987) p. 65.

17. Ibid, p. 64.

18. Ibid, p. 63.

19. Ibid, p. 62.

20. Piper, Joseph; Leisure: The Basic of culture (New York; The New American Library, Mentor Omega Books, 1963) p. 17.

21. Hingorani, Anand T; (ed), The Encyclopaedia of Gandhian Thoughts, (New Delhi; All India Congress Committee; 1985).

22. Harijan, Jan 28, 1939.

23. Ibid, May 5, 1946.

24. Ibid, April 20, 1934.

25. Ibid, May 5, 1946.

26. Ibid.

27. Ibid.

28. Ibid.

29. "Essential simplicity is the hallmark of Indian culture" – Harijan, Feb 18, 1939.

30. "Matter without spirit is dead and the spirit without matter cannot move. Each needs the help of others." – Collected works Mahatma Gandhi, (New Delhi; Vol. 2) p. 328.

31. "We may not attribute the weaknesses of the perishable body or the flesh to the imperishable soul that resides in it. We have to regulate the body in the light of the laws that govern the soul," Gandhi, To the women, (Karanchi; Anand T. Hingorani, 1941) p. 87.

32. "The forms are many but the informing spirit is one. How can there be room for distinction of high or low when there is this all – embracing fundamental unity underlying the outward diversity?" (Gandhi, Harijan,) Dec 15, 1933.

33. "The Gujarat Vidyapeeth does not propose merely to feed on or repeat the ancient cultures. It rather hopes to build a new culture based on the traditions of the past and enriched by the experience of later times. It stands for synthesis of different cultures that have come to stay in India, that have influenced Indian life and that in their turn, have themselves been influenced by the spirit of the soil. This synthesis will naturally be of the swadeshi type, where each culture is assured its legitimate place, and not of the American pattern where one dominant culture absorbs the rest, and where the aim is not towards harmony but towards an artificial and forced unity." – (Gandhi, Young India,) Nov 17, 1920.

34. Sri Aurbindo; The Foundations of Indian Culture, (Pondicherry: Sri Aurbindo Ashram,1959) p. 59.

35. Gandhi, M.K.; Hind Swaraj, p. 33.

36. Ibid, p. 24.

37. The Diary of Mahadeo Desai; p. 257.

38. Speeches and writings of Mahatma Gandhi (Madras; G.A. Nateshan, 1934) p. 1043.

39. Hind Swaraj, p. 37.

40. Ibid, p. 37.

41. Ibid, p. 33.

42. Gandhi, M.K; From Yarvada Mandir, p. 59.

43. Harijan, March 20, 1937.

44. Speeches and writings of Mahatma Gandhi, Opcit, p. 1042.

45. Young India, Oct 13, 1921.

46. Ibid, Dec, 8, 1927.

47. Ibid, Dec, 8, 1927.

48. Mukherjee, Radhakamal; The Sickness of Civilization, (Bombay; Allied Publishers 1964) p. 32.

49. Hind Swaraj, p. 39.

50. Ibid, p. 83.

51. Ibid, pp. 84- 85.

52. Ibid, pp. 55-56.

53. Speeches And Writings of Mahatma Gandhi, p. 97.

54. Harijan, Oct, 14, 1939.

55. Young India, March 17, 1927.

56. Harijan, Oct 14, 1939.

57. Ibid, Oct 14, 1939.

58. Hind Swaraj, p. 85.

59. Ibid, p. 49.

60. Ibid, pp. 53-54.

61. The Indian Review, Dec 1909, p. 134.

62. Young India, March 5, 1922.

63. Toynbee, Arnold; Mankind And Mother Earth, (New York; Oxford University Press 1976) p. 233.

64. Clough, Shepard. B; The Rise and Fall of Civilization, opcit, pp. 256-57.

65. Muller, Herbert; (1957) pp. 55-57.

66. Ikeda, Daisaku; "Modern civilization and Gandhism," Nanda, B.R. (ed.) Mahatma Gandhi , 125 years, (New Delhi; Indian council for cultural relations and New age international publishers, 1995) pp. 116-17.

67. Mahatma Gandhi, Vol. IX, Book II, The last phase Part I, pp. 234-35.

68. Ibid, p. 235.

69. Ibid, p. 235.

70. Ibid, p. 236.

71. Gandhi, M.K., Hind Swaraj or Indian Home Rule (Ahmedabad; Navajivan publishing House, 1938) (Revised edn 1939) p. 53.

72. Ibid, p. 53.

73. Ibid, p. 54.

74. Ibid, p. 56.

75. Ibid, p. 56.

76. Ibid, p. 68.

77. Ibid, p. 68.

78. Ibid, p. 69.

79. Ibid, p. 71.

80. Ibid, p. 77.

81. Ibid, p. 76.

82. Ibid, p. 76.

83. Ibid, p. 77.

84. Ibid, p. 77.

85. Young India, 12.11.1931, p. 335.

86. Ibid, 16.9.1926, p. 324.

87. Harijan, 11.8.1940, p. 245.

88. Ibid, 11.8.1940, p. 245.

89. Ibid, 11.8.1940, p. 245.

90. Young India, 1.10.1931, p. 286.

2

Truth and Non-Violence: The Foundation of Civilization

Every civilization has its root in its philosophy or metaphysics. Gandhism is not exception to it. It erects the whole structure of civilization on the twin principles of truth and non-violence. However, these concepts have broader meanings in Gandhism, hence, need explanation. Here we shall discuss first the concept of truth and then the concept of non-violence.

Concept of Truth

At the outset it is very pertinent to say that Gandhi was not an academic philosopher. He did not define the concept of truth sitting in the room or library. He used the concept in different senses as the result of his experimentation and enriched its denotation and meanings. This will be amply clear from this following statement:-

"Truth and non-violence are as old as the hills. All I have done is try experiments in both on as vast a scale as I could do."[1] "My faith in truth and non-violence is ever growing and as I am ever trying to follow them in my life, I too am growing every moment. I see new implications about them. I see them in a newer light every day and read in them a newer meaning."[2] Earlier in 1921, he said:-

"I represent no new truth. I endeavor to follow and represent truth as I know it. I do claim to throw a new light on many an old truth. I hope that this declaration will satisfy my inquirer and others like him."[3]

However, all this does not mean that the meanings and nature of Gandhi's truth will not be ascertained for cognitive purposes. His truth can be conceived from many angles of vision. Here we shall try to understand some of them.

(I) The Ontological meaning of Truth

Following the Indian vedantic tradition, Gandhi held truth as the Ultimate Reality. It is "Absolute Truth", "Sovereign Principle" or God. Etimologically, the equivalent of the word 'truth' is 'satya' derived from the word 'sat' which means 'being' or 'existence'. According to Gandhi, "Nothing is or exists in reality except Truth. That is why 'sat' or 'Truth' is perhaps the most important name of God. In fact, it is more correct to say that truth is God than to say that God is truth. But as we cannot do without a ruler or a general, such names of God as 'king of kings' or 'The Almighty' are and will remain generally current. On deeper thinking, however, it will be realized, that 'sat' or 'satya' is the only correct name and fully significant name of God."[4]

Truth is not separate from knowledge and bliss. It is also not distinct from good and beauty. Where there is truth or existence, knowledge is there and where there is knowledge, there is bliss also. Goodness cannot follow without truth and beauty should never be conceived devoid of truth. This is why God or Brahman or the Absolute is also characterized by 'Sachchidanand' i.e. truth, consciousness and bliss. He is also called 'Satyam, Shivam and Sundaram' – truth, goodness and beauty.

Gandhi makes a difference between the Absolute truth or God and the empirical truth which is called relative truth. The Absolute Truth is something unseen power beyond our perception. But the relative truths are the subject of our sense experience. Further, the Absolute truth is certain and eternal while the relative truths are transitory and uncertain. His following statements in this connection are worth seeing.

1. "There is an indefinable mysterious power that pervades everything. I feel it, though I do not see it. It is this unseen power which makes itself felt and yet defies all proof, because it is so unlike all that I perceive through my senses. It transcends the senses."[5]

2. "It is wrong to expect certainties in this world, where all else but God that is Truth is uncertainty. All that appears and happens about and around, is uncertain and transient. But there is a Supreme Being hidden therein as certainty and one would be blessed, if one could catch a glimpse of that Certainty. The quest of that truth is the Summum Bonum of life."[6]

3. "God is not a power residing in the clouds. God is an unseen power residing within us and nearer to us than finger nails to the flesh. There are many powers lying hidden within us and we discover them by constant struggle. Even so we may find this supreme power if we make diligent search with the fixed determination to find Him."[7]

The transitoriness of the world does not lead Gandhi to call it unreal, for the foundation of it is eternal. If 'eternality' is 'real' and 'changing unreal', world is both real and unreal. He believes in the theory of points of view and manyness of Reality.

1. "I am always true from my point of view and am often wrong from the point of view of my honest critics. I know that we are both right from our respective points of view."[8]

2. "From the platform of the Jains, I prove the non-creative aspect of God and from that of Ramanuja, the creative aspect. As a matter of fact we are all thinking of the unthinkable, describing the undescribable, seeking to know the unknown and that is why our speech falters, is inadequate and even often contradictory."[9]

The truth by nature is self-evident and also self-illuminating. When the ignorance surrounding our mind is removed, it becomes illumined to us.

1. "Truth is by nature self-evident. As soon as you remove the cobwebs of ignorance that surround it, it shines clear."[10]

2. "Every expression of truth has in it the seeds of propagation, even as the sun cannot hide its light."[11]

To Gandhi, truth is not only God but sovereign principle of the world, which includes all the principles or laws of the creation. "Truth is 'the sovereign principle', which includes numerous other principles. This truth is not only truth fullness in words but truth fullness in thought also and not only the relative truth of our conception, but 'The Absolute Truth', the eternal principle, that is God."[12]

Epistemological meaning of Truth

We have seen that Gandhi's truth is not only absolute existence but also absolute knowledge which is self-evident. All the knowledge of the world is derived from the absolute. But question is how one can know the truth? Gandhi answers this question with the help of conscience of the individual. Answering to the question what is truth, in Switzerland Gandhi said: "Truth is what the voice within tells you"[13] This voice is called 'Voice of God', 'Voice of conscience', 'Voice of Truth', 'inner voice' or 'The still small voice'.[14] He also suggested to call it 'dictates of reason'.[15] Generally, sense perception and reason are known to be the source of knowledge. However, these are unable to give us the knowledge of truth. It is intuition alone through which the knowledge of truth or spiritual knowledge becomes possible. The inner voice is intuitive knowledge, but not in the sense of mystic realization of 'soul', 'Brahman' or 'Nirvana'. It is knowledge which guides us in given situation. It is not necessary that every one's 'inner voice' be the same as we find in mystic realization of the saints. But every one is capable of hearing this voice if he or she fulfils the conditions required for it which we shall discuss later on. Gandhi said: "Truth resides in every human heart and one has to search for it there and to be guided by truth as one sees it. But no one has right to coerce others to act according to his own view of truth."[16] "There is nothing wrong in everyone following according to his light."[17]

However, Gandhi's 'inner voice' raised several criticisms. It is argued that however sincere one may be striving towards truth, difference is a certainty which will lead to chaos in society. If there is difference between the truths of two persons, who will settle the issue? Even robbers and murderers would also claim that they act according to their own truth. Gandhi answered that "in resolving conflicts of truths between the two persons, individual alone is capable to resolve the conflict. No third party is needed to resolve it. So far the question of differences in truths is concerned, it is natural and the problem will be solved with the help of Ahimsa."[18] The wrong doers cannot justify their acts in the name of their 'inner voice', because they have not gone under training to acquire it. Gandhi is very clear that in the name of 'false claimants', the 'inner voice' cannot and ought not be suppressed. If inner voice is truthfully represented, there is no danger, however, "There is no remedy of hypocrisy".[19]

In modern western logic and philosophy, truth is property of proposition. A proposition may be true or false. An argument may be valid and invalid and two propositions may be consistent and inconsistent. With regard to 'truth' three theories-correspondent theory, coherence theory and pragmatic theory are known to us. If a proposition is according to the fact outside-that is if idea corresponds to the reality, it is called correspondence theory of truth. If two propositions are consistent in a given universe – the theory is called coherence theory of truth and if a belief or proposition works or brings expected result, it is called pragmatic theory.

Gandhi's truth is not the property of a proposition, it is attribute of God and Soul and matter of gradual realization. Those who believe in consistency as essence of truth are wrong as it goes against the creativity and evolution of truth. Many critics of the West charge Gandhi to be inconsistent in his 'voice of truth'. Mr. Erik H. Erikson writes – "Compared with the charismatic men of his time Gandhi and his 'inner-voice' may seen more moodily, personal, more mystically religions and more formless in ideology than any of them. There is nothing more consistent in the views of Gandhi's critics than the accusation of inconsistency; At one time he is accused of sounding like a socialist and at another a dreamy conservative, or again a pacifist and a frentic militarist; a nationalist and a communalist; an anarchist and a devotee of tradition; a western activist and an Easter mysticist; a total religionist and yet so liberal that he could say he saw God even in the atheist's atheism. Did this polymorphous man have a firm centre?"[20]

But this charge is wrong as there is 'category mistake'. Gandhi never bothered about the consistency between what he said earlier and what he says now. There is a different meaning of 'consistency' in his philosophy which is very much near to Judaism and The Old Testament. "For the earlier Judaism, 'truth' meant consistency or faith fullness – the meaning is ethical." In the Old Testament... "truth means that which is consistent with itself, loyal to its own nature". Obviously consistency is applied with the person, not with the proposition. Gandhi also thinks of consistency in what one thinks, speaks and does. The nature of 'consistency' in his thought and action will be amply clear from his following statements:-

1. "I decline to be slave to precedents or practice I cannot understand or defend on a moral basis".[21]

2. "I must admit my many in consistencies. But since I am called 'Mahatma' I might well endorse Emerson's saying that foolish consistency is the hobgoblin of little minds. There is, I fancy, a method in my inconsistencies. In my opinion, there is a consistency running through my seeming inconsistencies, as in Nature there is unity running through seeming diversity".[22]

3. "Inconsistency is only apparent. It appears so to many friends because of my responsiveness to varying circumstances. Seeming consistency may really be sheer obstinacy".[23]

4. "I am not at all concerned with appearing to be consistent... what I am concerned with is my readiness to obey the call of truth, my God, from moment to moment".[24]

5. "I have never made a fetish of consistency. I am votary of truth and I must say what I feel and think at a given moment on the question, with out regard to what I may have said before on it... As my vision gets clearer, my views must grow clearer with daily practice. Where I have deliberately altered my opinion. The change should be

obvious, only a careful eye would notice a gradual and imperceptible evolution."[25]

6. "My aim is not to be consistent with my previous statements on a given question, but to be consistent with truth as it may present itself to me at a given moment. The result has been that I have grown from truth to truth".[26]

7. "I would like to say to the diligent reader of my writings and to others who are interested in them that I am not at all concerned with appearing to be consistent. In my search after truth I have discarded many ideas and learnt many new things. Therefore, when any body finds any inconsistency between any two writings of mine, if he has still faith in my sanity, he would do well to choose the later of the two on the same subject."[27]

The above statements show Gandhi's aversion towards verbal or propositional consistency. He did not want to be the 'slave of precedent'. 'Seeming consistency is sheer obstinacy', it is 'hobgoblin of little mind' and is against the evolution of truth realization as well as creativity of truth. The real consistency consists in obeying the call of the truth in given situation in the ambit of truth and non-violence. The changes in statements made by Gandhi did not cross the border of truth and non-violence. The changes are due to progress in his realization. He grew from truth to truth and hence, suggested to choose the later statements on the subject. The real test of his consistency lies in what he thought, he propagated and lived accordingly – that is consistency in his character. Therefore, if one wants to seek propositional consistency in his truth, it will be just like to ask why a cow is not buffalo. Gandhi's consistency will be appreciated when one will minutely observe the inner harmony among his ideas of different field of life. It is due to inner harmony in his thoughts and actions which distinguished him from the other great men and saints of the world. Last but not the least; he will ever remain consistent so long there are untruth, violence and injustice on earth.

The ethical meaning of Truth

Truth is not only existence, knowledge but also morality. When Gandhi prescribes five vows including truth, he means by 'truth' a moral concept. It is moral aspect of truth which impressed Gandhi from his very childhood. As all of us know that he refused to take prompt by his teacher, when he misspelt the word 'kettle' during visit of school inspector Mr. Giles. We also know that the play, Harishchandra which he saw in his childhood, 'captured his heart'. 'Lives and examples of Harishchandra, Prahlad, Ramchandra, Imam Hassan and Imam Hussain, the Christian saints' – remained ideal of his life. "How beautiful it would be, if all of us, men and women, devoted ourselves wholly to truth in all that we might do in our waking hours, whether working, eating, drinking or playing, till dissolution of the body makes us one with truth"- he exclaimed.[28] But what is moral truth? Moral truth is not only the accuracy of speech, but a symmetry of thinking, speaking and doing – one in 'mansa , bacha and karmana'. Here he defers from the view point of ancient Hebrews to whom "truth was a matter of motive and character, rather than of accuracy". To Christ "truth meant consistency of character; it was truth of action rather than truth of ideas".[29] However, in Gandhi's 'truth' consistency of character means 'oneness in motive, speech and action'. No part is left in the total sense of 'Truth'. He writes: - "Generally speaking, observation of the law of truth is understood merely to mean that we must speak the truth. But we in the Ashram should understand the word 'satya' or 'truth' in a much wider sense. There should be truth in thought, truth in speech and truth in action. To the man who has realized this truth in its fullness, nothing else remains to be known, because all knowledge is necessarily included in it".[30]

According to Gandhi this holistic Truth is the supreme value of human life. He said; "Devotion to this truth is the sole justification for our existence. All our activities should be the very breath of our life. When once this stage in the pilgrims progress is reached, all other rules of correct living will come without effort and obedience to them will be instinctive".[31]

Gandhi's truth is a purifying concept. It not only purifies individual's heart but has also ability to purify the social, political, economic and other environment in which human beings live. "A merely personal and private holiness indifferent to public morality, is to him unthinkable" and perhaps here he is original. What is true for the individual is also true for society, he believed. This led him to enter into politics. He moralized and spiritualized politics. "My devotion to truth which has drawn me into the field of politics; and I can say without slightest of hesitation; and yet in all humility, that those who say that religion has nothing to do with politics do not know what religion means." "Politics bereft of religion are absolute dirt ever to be shunned" – he said. Obviously here by religion, he means 'Truth' and 'Non-violence'. He applied 'truth' in politics in the form of open diplomacy, 'satyagraha', a technique of settling political and social wrongs, unilateralism, the concept of non-violent state and purity of end and means – both in politics- a novel thing and very distinct from the politics of today based on untruth.

He lived the life of truth and advocated to be truthful in legal profession also, in contrary to the view of an English lawyer "that it may be the duty of an advocate to defend a client whom he knows to be guilty". Gandhi said, "The duty of a lawyer is always to place before the judges and help them to arrive at the truth, never to prove guilty as innocent". It was his conviction that, "it was not impossible to practise law without compromising truth". In his own practice in South Africa, Gandhi resisted the temptation to encourage his own client or witness to lie even though by the suppression or adornment of the truth, he would win his case. Once, when it came to his notice that his client had deceived him, he asked the magistrate to withdraw the case. "In my hearts of heart, I always wished that I should win only if my client's case was right." – This was his stand in his legal profession.

In the matter of commerce which is known for untruth, Gandhi advised to be truthful. He wanted to transform business relation "by sincere loyalty to truth". He believed that in the delicate business of personal relation, a complete openness and devotion to truth would clear up a thousand problems. In his personal life, he was very much particular in maintaining the accounts of expenditure of public fund.

In public life, Gandhi's preaching always accompanied his living. He gave a call of swadeshi against the British exploitation of India economy and began spinning and wear khadi. He championed the cause of scheduled castes and accordingly lived in the 'Harijan Basti'. He stood for the downtrodden and clad himself as the poor in India live. He would travel in the third class- the class of general people. All this shows the truth for him was a living principle. This is also in contrast with the living and preaching of the modern leaders, who champion the cause of democracy and act as autocrats claim to be the leaders of backward and scheduled castes and live an aristocratic life. Last but not the least, Gandhi opted martyrdom for the cause of truth and non-violence –what was his religion and conviction. This testifies his sincerity in the moral concept of his truth.

Truth as a working principle of life

Gandhi's truth is not only metaphysical, epistemological and moral; it has a special meaning which may be termed a 'working principle' or a life style leading towards moral and spiritual progress through day-today life. It is a principle which can be practiced by all, just contrary to the view of Clement- a western 'truth mystic' to whom the knowledge of deepest thing like truth is possible to the few only. In Gandhian principle, "what is possible for one is possible for all", even for a child. It is truth as a life style which elevated Mohandas to Mahatma Gandhi, recognized by the whole world. He symbolized greatness and goodness together. In the history of the concept of truths, he distinguished himself with this special aspect of truth. Verrier Elvin rightly observed: - "His conception of truth is metaphysical, mystical and moral; there is no aspect of it which is not real to him. It has been his special task to bring this lofty philosophical idea down to earth to introduce it as a working principle into the lives of ordinary people, to direct its austere moral challenge upon world politics, to exalt it is as a practical basis of business and personal relations and to workout with great exactness, what is implied in the quest for its realization." However, Gandhi's truth is not only the working principle of outward life alone which is visible to the world. He made truth working principle of spiritual or internal life too which is not public. He wrote: - "my experiments in the political field are now known, not only in India, but to a certain extent to the civilized world... But I should certainly like to narrate my experiments in the spiritual field which are known only to myself and from which I have derived such power as I possess for working in the political field." "There are some things which are known only to oneself and one's maker. They are clearly incommunicable." But he experimented, rather applied truth in this field also and made its result public, how much immoral and unpleasing they might be. This experiment provided him moral and spiritual strength and gave him satisfaction and peace even in committing 'Himalayan Blunder' or in the state of 'canker of untruth'. In his Autobiography, he disclosed how he could conquer his evils with the help of truth. To him truth was a method of self-correction. 'Self-correction' and 'self-purification' were identical to him. He wanted to purify individual and his surroundings adhering to truth. Self-purification means, "to become absolutely passion-free in thought, speech and action; to rise above the opposing currents of love and hatred, attachment and repulsion." To conquer subtle passion is "harder far than the pnysical conquest of the world by the force of arms." Therefore, one cannot claim that he has won his passions completely. But by humility, constant effort, confession, sincere repentance, transparancy and open mind, one can certainly contain his passions to a great extent and have a glimpse of absolute Truth in the progress from truth to truth.

In the pretext of modern self-deceptive and hypocritical civilization, this aspect of Gandhi's truth can be a panacea of all the ills. Modern man looks outward to show himself civilized. But true civilization consists in the inner growth of man. To appear good outward and conceal the evil within – are the major diseases in the progress of morality and spirituality; causing peacelessness in human beings. In a true civilization, outlook should be changed. Gandhi showed to the world that truth must be a guide in every step of life. If truth is applied in day today's life, man will certainly grow in higher power of truth and morality. If any body practices this aspect of truth, he will elevate himself to the highest position of life- the life eternal.

Realization of Truth

At the outset, I want to make it clear that 'truth' and 'God' are not identical terms. If identical, God means some thing different from the traditional theistic conception of God. G. Ramchandran observes: - "Truth is not just fact but fact is in the truth. One both speaks the truth and acts the truth. When Gandhi speaks in term of God, he means immanent God present and vibrant in every atom of the universe, self-evolving from within, guiding, directing and growing. It is this God that becomes truth. The whole process of cosmic life gets embedded in the idea of Gandhi's truth." In this sense Gandhi used both the terms 'truth realization' and 'God realization' in the same sense. Broadly speaking, in Gandhian scheme of thought, Truth is revealed through non-violence, as the former is the end and the later means. Because we shall discuss non-violence in the 2nd part of this discussion. Let us be satisfied here with some of the other virtues essential for the realization of value truth-metaphysical, ethical, epistemological, practical even scientific taken together.

Humility is of paramount importance in the quest of truth. "Truth without humility would be an arrogant caricature", Gandhi said.[32] For "no one can see God face to face who has caught of the I in him. He must become a cipher if he would see God. Who shall dare saying in this stormed-tossed universe, I have won? God triumphs in us, never we."[33] In 1931 he further said, "Truth is not to be found by any body who has not got an abundant sense of humility. If you would swim on the bosom of the ocean of truth, you must reduce yourself to zero."[34] In his Autobiography he observed, "The seeker after truth should be humbler than the dust. The world crushes the dust under its feet, but the seeker after truth should so humble himself that even the dust could crush him".[35] In the last of the Autobiography he concluded, "So long as a man does not of his own free will put himself last among his fellow creatures, there is no salvation for him. Ahimsa is the farthest limit of humility".[36] Pride and arrogance are great barrier in the quest of truth. The Mahatma said, "To feel that we are something is to setup a barrier between God and ourselves; to cease feeling that we are something is to become one with God. A drop in the ocean partakes of the greatness of its parent although it is unconscious of it. But it is dried up as soon as it enters upon an existence independent of the ocean."[37] However, he warns that humility should not be taken in the sense of 'inertia'. "True humility means most strenuous and constant endeavour entirely directed towards the service of humanity" and "a life of service must be one of humility".[38] "Because God is continuously in action without resting for a single moment."[39] "He will be realized by patient endeavour and silent prayer."[40] "When we cease to be masters and reduce ourselves to the rank of servants, humbler than the very dust under our feet, all fears will roll away like mists, we shall attain ineffable peace and see Satyanarayan (The God of Truth) face to face."

It is not Gandhi alone who highlighted the role of humility in the quest of truth, but many of the western 'truth mystics' also held the same view. Walter Hiltom said, "Truth and Humility are true sisters, fastened together in love and charity." St. Bernard, emphasizing the importance of humility in quest of truth wrote: - "By the tears of penitence, by the pursuit of righteousness and by persistence in works of mercy, is the spiritual sight cleared from all stains; and to it Truth promises to reveal itself in its purity. There are thus, three degrees of truth. We rise to the first by humble effort, to the second by loving sympathy, to the third by enraptured vision. In the first, truth is revealed in severity, in the second in pity, in the third in purity. Reason by which we analyse ourselves, guides us to the first, feeling which enables us to have compassion on others, conducts us to the second, purity by which we are raised to the level of the unseen, carries us up to the third." (P.6) Gandhi did not talk about the degrees of truth. He believed in integral truth and hence, every step of realization of truth is important in the quest of absolute truth as well as relative truths. Self-analysis, purity and feeling of service are essential for both the spiritual as well as scientific truths. In all kinds of quest of truth, we need to have an attitude to see things as they are. And this requires humility in its fullness. "When self-satisfaction creeps over a man, he has ceased to grow and therefore become unfit for freedom"[41] – that is truth.

The second virtue, indispensable for the quest of truth, is fearlessness. A coward cannot be truthful and non-violent. This is the reason that Gandhi included fearlessness, among the six cardinal moral virtues essential for the Satyagrahi. A Satyagrahi has to observe eleven vows of truth, non-violence, non-stealing, celibacy, non-possession, bread labour, non-satisfying of palate, fearlessness, equal respect to all religions, swadeshi and touchability. Among all these, four are of spatio-temporal relevance and one i.e. non-satisfying of palate essential for observing celibacy. However, six moral virtues-truth, non-violence, non-stealing, non-possession, celibacy and fearlessness are relevant for all and all the times.

Fearlessness is indispensable for the seeker of truth and non-violence and "Fearlessness connotes freedom from all external fear-fear of disease, bodily injury and death, of dispossession, of losing one's nearest and dearest, of losing reputation or giving offence and so on."[42] "The pursuit of truth is true devotion- the path that leads to God. Therefore, there is no room for cowardishness and defeat in it." "Fearlessness is the first requisite for spirituality. Cowards can never be moral."[43] Further, "fearlessness is indispensable for the growth of other noble qualities. How can one seek truth or cherish love, without fearlessness,"[44] he asks. In fact, satyagraha demands sacrifice and "in true sacrifice, all the suffering is on one side-one is required to master the art of getting killed without killing."[45] "Satyagrahi must stand unmoved in the midst of all cross currents."[46]"Nothing better can happen to a satyagrahi than meeting death all unsought in the very act of satyagraha, i.e. pursuing truth."[47] All this means that a seeker after truth must be ready to suffer all the ordeals inflicted upon him by those who live in untruth and it requires fearlessness.

According to Swami Vivekananda the realization of the ultimate truth, is possible either of the four paths – the path of knowledge, the path of action, the path of devotion and the path of meditation. Gandhi believed in the path of selfless service to humanity – a path which synthesizer both path of action and devotion in itself. He had perhaps no leaning towards the path of knowledge and meditation. He argued, "Man's ultimate aim is the realization of God and all his activities, social political religious have to be guided by the ultimate aim of the vision of God. The immediate service of all human beings becomes a necessary part of the endeavour, simply because the only way to find God is to see Him in his creation and be one with it. This can only be done by service of all . I am a part and parcel of the whole and I cannot find Him apart from rest of the humanity."[48] Further, "man becomes great exactly in the degree in which he works for the welfare of his fellow-men".[49]

To Gandhi, service without selflessness, has no meaning and to serve without desire is the duty of human beings. He advocated, "To serve without desire is to favour not others, but ourselves, even as in discharging a debt, we serve only ourselves, lighten our burden and fulfil our duty. Again not only the good, but all of us are bound to place our resources at the disposal of humanity. The duty of renunciation differentiates mankind from the beast."[50] Like other Indian philosopher Gandhi also held that human being can not be free from the cycle of rebirth, unless he gives up all attachments to the body. "This freedom from all attachments is the realization of God as truth. Such realization cannot be attained in a hurry."[51]

Modern civilization is the civilization of din and bustle in which truth realization is difficult. Truth realization needs silence.

Truth

Truth is the ultimate Reality in Gandhism. Generally understood, ultimate Reality is that which can explain every thing of the universe. To Gandhi, it is not enough. The ultimate Reality should also satisfy the divergent faiths of human beings and it should be capable of applying in every field of life as well as restructuring society on its foundation. In the West materialism, idealism and neutralism are different ontological theories, which are extremes and incapable of satisfying the every psychological entity. Further, on their basis, no sound society can be restructured. In India there is integralism of Sri Aurobindo, which can be claimed to be a fine synthesis of all the extremes. However, it cannot satisfy the analytical mind and therefore, it is not tried in building up of the society. But Gandhi's truth explains all the realities, satisfies both the theists and the atheists and can be applied in reshaping the different structures of society – economic, political, social, educational as well as defensive.

References

1. Harijan, 28.3.1936.
2. Harijan, 2.3.1940.
3. Young India, 25.8.1921, p. 267.
4. Yarvada Mandir, chapt-I.
5. Young India, 11.10.1928.
6. My Experiments with Truth, 2nd edn. 1940, p. 184.
7. Harijan, 28.3.1953.
8. Young India, 21.01.1926.
9. Young India 21.01.1926.
10. Young India 27.5.1926, p. 189.
11. The Modern Review, Oct; 1935, p. 413.
12. 26.11.1925 in the introduction of My Experiments with Truth, 2004, p. XI.
13. Young India, 31.12.1931.
14. Harijan, 7.8.1933.
15. The Bombay Chronicles, 18.11.1933.

16. Harijan, 24.11.1933, p. 6.
17. Yarvada Mandir, p. 4.
18. Young India, 1919-22, published in Book form by Tagore & co Madras, 1922, p. 29.
19. Harijan, 18.3.1933.
20. Gandhi's truth on the origins of Militant Non-violence, pp. 395-96.
21. Young India, 27.7.1921, p. 228.
22. Ibid, 13.2.1930, p. 52.
23. Ibid, 16.4.1931, p. 77.
24. Harijan, 29.4.1933, p. 2.
25. Harijan, 28.9.1934, p. 260.
26. Harijan, 30.9.1939. p. 288.
27. Harijan, 29.4.1933, p. 2.
28. Yarvada mandir, chap. I.
29. The modern Review, 1933, p. 3.
30. M.K.Gandhi, Truth is God, pp. 19-20.
31. Ibid, p. 20.
32. Young India, 25.6.1925.
33. Ibid.
34. Young India, 31.12.1931.
35. Autobiography, Introduction, p. XII.
36. Ibid, p. 420.
37. Yarvada Mandir, p. 68.

38. Ibid, p. 68.
39. Ibid, p. 68.
40. Young India, 1.6.1921, p. 174.
41. Young India, 29.9.1921, p. 306.
42. Yarvada Mandir, p. 41.
43. Young India, 13.10.21, p. 323.
44. Yarvada Mandir, p. 40.
45. Young India, 8.5.1930, p. 161.
46. Ibid, 4.6.25, p. 189.
47. S.F.G. P. 244 originally in. S.A.P. 288 Ist edn S.A. Ganeshan Madras 1928 2nd edn Navajivan 1950.
48. Harijan, 29.8.1936, p. 226.
49. Ethical Religion, 1930 S. Ganeshan Madras, p. 56.
50. Yarvada Mandir, p. 81.
51. Yarvada Mandir, Chap II.

3

Civilizational Crisis and Beyond

Man, Society and Nature are facing such an unprecedented predicament in the present "satanic civilization" that their better existence has become impossible nay existence itself has reached on the throes of annihilation. The civilization which encircles us is essentially materialistic. Science, heavy industries, commercialism, market economy, excessive reliance on dehumanized technology, city-life, consumerism, power oriented politics and division in every walk of social life are its main components. There is no room for religion, morality, spirituality and self-restraint in it and consequently, the inner life of man is being eroded in absence of proper nourishment. Indiscriminate "rape of the earth", environmental pollution, growing warming of the atmosphere, self-alienation, direct and indirect forms of violence and mass unemployment have resulted in to all encompassing peacelessness in modern Society.

We are facing a wide range of crisis engulfing each and every aspect of life. Inspite of the materialistic pursuits masses are suffering from the object poverty and unemployment and hence there is economic crisis. The world is hankering after development, but the society is being diseased of maldevelopment. There is crisis of ecological imbalances. Human aspect of our personality is waning day by day. There is moral crisis resulting in the crisis of character. The youngsters badly face the crisis of value to be opted in life. There is spiritual crisis or crisis of faith badly affecting human relations. But above all there is only one crisis and that is civilizational crisis adversely affecting our cultural life.

Broadly speaking, the term civilization refers to (i) The concept of progress of development. (ii) A certain mode of life which binds the people of a group or nation or international community. In fact, a mode of life is interlinked with the concept of progress. As is our idea of progress, so becomes our life-style. Both are so interrelated that they cannot be separated from each other.

In using the term civilizational crisis, we mean 'Civilization' in the sense of modern civilization which believes in material progress as only mark of civilization. In the thread of material progress, it tries to weave out the individual as well as social development.

Sometimes, 'civilization' and 'culture' are used synonymously. In Indian philosophies 'culture' and 'civilization' are used as identical. Maharshi Aurbindo and Mahatma Gandhi, very candidly used them in identical sense.[1] However, in western social sciences, both the terms are distinguished from one another. According to the western anthropologists and behavior scientists, a culture is the behavior pattern of a group of people. Thus, being the behavior pattern of a group, culture is applicable only for a group, not for an individual. But in Indian philosophies, culture is applicable for both, individual and society, facts and values, inner and outer qualities of man. Gandhi talked of 'culture of mind', 'culture of heart' and inner and outer culture.

We find the following relations between the two concepts:-

1. From the Indian point of view, civilization and culture both are identical and all inclusive of our consciousness.

2. From western point of view, they are different yet related with each other. Taken in to account the ancient western meaning of civilization, it becomes a type of culture and therefore, is included in the concept of culture. Sometimes, distinction is made by describing civilization as external progress and means of achievements and culture as internal enlightenment and end in itself. However, it cannot be taken to be true as reality is the whole and hence it is futile to draw line between the internal and external and between means and end.

3. Used in the modern sense, civilization is the whole and culture its parts. The Civilization is the symbol of whole of material and social progress where as culture refers to the behavioural and life style aspect of civilization.

4. It is held that 'civilization' is a concept which is related to change and modernity where as culture is concerned with tradition and continuity. But this distinction is not tenable as both being social phenomena are subject of tradition and continuity, change and modernity.

5. Rene Dubos one of the pioneers of environmental studies, distinguishes civilization from culture by using 'civilization' in the singular when referring to the values that can be shared and are increasingly shared by most people irrespective of origin race of religion.

In contrast, 'culture' is the plural to designate the body of values, ideas and beliefs which are characteristics of a particular group.[2] Dr. Mourad Wahaba also shares his view.

Factually, this distinction seems to be true albeit in the ideal or normative sense both civilization and culture are one. From the aforesaid distinction, it may tentatively be concluded that civilization covers comparatively larger space and time while cultures are localized. Most of the international communities developed or undeveloped, believe in one and only one civilization which is materialistic though their culture vary due to different geography and traditions. Civilization is measured in the scale of age but culture in the scale of period.

Civilizational Crisis

All the crisis experienced in the modern world, can be explained in terms of civilizational crisis. Therefore, in a sense, it is metaphysical in nature. To make it more clear it can be said that our wrong and inadequate notion of progress or development is the cause of crisis in every walk of life. Theories of development capitalistic or socialistic or Nehruvian are one sided and wrong as they are essentially materialistic. No development models believe in all round development because maldevelopment causes multiple crisis in modern society. The maldevelopment disintegrated man, society as well as nature and brought human civilization on cross-road. For the natural growth of civilization, a balanced and harmonious relation between the different aspect of life is essential, failing which predicamental situations arise in the entire activities of so called civilized people.

The present civilization is responsible for the 'divide within social setting such as family, village, town, ethnic groups and communities'. It has created splits in them and eroded communitarian life. K.D. Gangrade rightly remarks, "The present political and development process are acting as catalyst of a collective decadence. A society which lays emphasis more on the accumulation of power than on the restraints, on wealth than on morality, on knowledge than on humanism and demagogy rather than on authentic sharing and participation in the process of change and development, is bound to pay heavy price for lack of collective wisdom".[3]

The damaging fissures in society are not due to outward forces but are pregnant within the civilization, causing serious crisis in social life.

The morality and spirituality of social being depend upon the structure of society he lives in as well as the philosophy and end which a society seeks to realize. With the split and violent structure and materialistic and utilitarian goal, the present civilization cannot lead humanity ahead towards peace and happiness. It is bound to create a moral and spiritual chaos in human society. Today we see multiple faces of violence, unrest distrust and loss of faith in interpersonal and inter group relations. Corruption and immorality are the special features of developed and developing society. All this proves the decadence of higher moral and spiritual values.

Though, the civilization is committed to rapid economic growth through industrialization, yet it is incompetent to deliver even material well-beings to all. Firstly, there is no logical connection between economic growth and alleviation of poverty. John Robinson rightly pointed out – "a growth in wealth is not at all the same thing as reducing poverty- as growth goes on at the top, more and more families are thrown out at the bottom. Absolute misery grows while wealth increase".[4] In fact affluence can never guarantee equal and equitable distribution of income and wealth. Therefore, despite the significant economic growth, most of the people in the world are living in grinding poverty. Secondly, the present model of economic development contains inherent contradiction and hence never be a sustainable model of development. The economic development absolutely based on heavy industries and unrenewable energy as well as abuse of land, can never last long. From some corner, efforts are being made to make it sustainable with the help of renewable and non-exhaustible energy. But it is not solution of the real problem. In true sense of the term, a sustainable development refers to human development which is lacking in the existing model. The economic development is the means to develop the whole facilities of human beings which is possible only in participatory involvement of the people in economic activities. A sustainable development is really based on its moral, spiritual and just social foundations. Dr. R.P. Mishra rightly remarks - "Sustainability is multifaceted. When seen in parts and out side the context of the whole, it loses its real meaning".[5] The unjust and unsustainable economic development is, in fact, economic crisis or crisis in development caused by modern civilization itself.

The modern civilization has not only affected our socio-economic and ethico-spiritual systems adversely, but the whole of eco system also. The greedy civilization depleted earth and polluted the whole of atmosphere, lithosphere and hydrosphere and is also responsible for the degradation of biosphere. Many species of the animals and birds of the planet are diminishing day by day. There is danger of green house effect and ozone holes in the atmosphere, resulting in excess warming and rising of sea levels. The all round pollution has generated many types of disease in man and other species. In short, there is crisis in nature.

The crisis in nature is due to wrong relation established between man and nature by modern civilization. The Indian wisdom is to live friendly with nature like a family member. But the civilization-product of Western wisdom, regards nature as foe and the object to be vanquished and exploited for the pleasure of man. The hedonist civilization went such an extent in exploitation of nature that it has become diseased and proceeding towards bankruptcy rapidly. No doubt the environmentalists are involved in seeking solution of the problem but they are medicines of the ailments, not the cure of disease. All the problems of nature are infact problem with the civilization and ecological crisis is fundamentally civilizational crisis. Unless and until the efforts, to go beyond the civilization, is made, the crisis in nature will go deeper and deeper and very existence on planet will meet disaster.

Civilizational crisis is also the cause of cultural crisis in society. It is pertinent to distinguish here, the difference between civilizational crisis and cultural crisis. The civilizational crisis means the worng in the very concept of civilization which results in to all round crisis in society, while cultural crisis means the crisis in human behaviours, style of living and in all behavioural institutions etc. In a cultural crisis, there is loss of spirit in human personality and lack of purpose in social institutions. Love, compassion, co-operation and feeling to serve others are some of the qualities of soul which serve as cementing force in society and liberating force in human life. But these are overshadowed in the dazzling materialism of the civilization. The materialistic values have become so powerful that even an aspirant of morality and noble actions fail in finding out the suitable path of life. The purpose of politics is to give good management to people; the purpose of religion is to unite with the transcendental values. But the politics, education and religions have become meaningless in the unlimited hunger of material pleasure in the present civilization. In fact, all the crisis are symptoms and civilization is disease. Knowing the symptoms we must try to get out of the disease and enjoy the happiness of all round peaceful life.

How to go beyond the crisis

The crucial problem before modern man is how to get rid of this monster. Civilization is not like a clock which can be put on and put off at wishes. It is a product of long process, hence, its containment is a wise step with firm belief and enduring patience. One cannot come out of civilization at once alone. It would be as suicidal as jumping out from the running express train. If we want to disembark from the train we will have to wait for the coming station or request the guard and the driver to stop the train. Similarly if we sincerely want to get out of the present civilization, we should have the vision of true civilization and leaders of the world in different fields, i.e. politics, economics, religion and society as a whole will have to come forward. The leaders would first have to live themselves in accordance with the alternative true civilization and then disseminate the ideas among their followers to motivate them as Mahatma Gandhi did.

But the question is, what is a true civilization to be cultivated to avert the crisis? To me it seems, Mahatma Gandhi is the beacon light in this regard. It can be said that his ideas of decentralization of all kinds of powers, labour and mass oriented ecocomic growth based on eco-friendly technology and purity of means, simple living and high thinking as the motto of individual and social life, all round development and liberation of human personality and society, synthesis of science and spirituality in different walks of life, life affirming and dynamic spirituality, cultural mutuality and dialogues, ethical religions and appliance of moral power or soul force in resolving all kind of conflicts will have to be zealously followed. These principles are not only object of noble thoughts to be widely disseminated but also the guiding principles of re-structuring socio-economic and political structures of the present day society.

If needed, the political leaders of the world meet together and discuss the model of new civilization in the line of Gandhian principles and also build a consensus of implementing strategies. The conscious people of the world should come forward to educate people in new civilization.

Thus, with the help of Gandhian principles and their people's education along with the non-violent structures of society we may smoothly go beyond the present day's civilizational crisis. Toynbee, the eminent historian rightly remarked, "It is becoming clear that a chapter which had a western beginning will have to have an Indian ending if it is not to end in the self destruction of the human race."[6]

References

1. Mahatma Gandhi in "Hind Swaraj" and Sri Aurbindo in "The foundation of Indian culture", used the term civilization identically.

2. Wahaba, Mourad; ed; Cultures in conflict or in Dialogue (Cario: Proceedings of third Afro Asian Ahilogophy conference 1990) p.108.

3. Singh, Ramjee; ed; Gandhi And the Future of Humanity (Varanasi. Gandhian Institute of Studies,1977) p. 84.

4. Ibid, p. 90.

5. Ibid, p. 113.

6. Singh, Ramjee; Gandhi and the Twenty-first Century (New Delhi; Peace Publishers, 1993) p. 86.

4

Gandhi and the Concept of Structural Violence

In the history of human culture and civilization it was perhaps Mahatma Gandhi who for the first time could see the vast ocean of violence inherent in present social structures of different societies of the world and above all in the modern western civilization. He was the first spiritualist who broke the shackles of nonviolence which was caged under the false notion of personal morality and suppressed by inactivity and other worldliness of the life of a recluse and made it an all-comprehensive subject of social life and sociology. Hence there is no wonder if he could inspire John Galtung, a world leader of peace researchers and non violent sociology. In the preface to his book 'Buddhism; A Quest for Unity and Peace', Johan Galtung writes, "Gandhi was an eye-opener to me...But the influence Gandhi had on me as a peace researcher went far beyond these efforts to explore Gandhi's own thought and action. Gandhi's optimism, that it is possible to overcome violence with nonviolent means, and his profound structuralism, putting the blame of the wrong structure rather than the evil actor, in addition to his spiritualism, were major sources of inspiration for all my latter efforts, to come to grips with violence of various kinds, direct, structural or cultural."[1]

The Concept of Structural Violence

Violence, in contemporary world phenomena, has assumed different connotations and meanings. It is not merely killing, inflicting injury or domination over others by a person or group. Galtung says: "Violence is present when human beings are being influenced so that their actual somatic and mental realizations are below their potential realizations."[2] "Anything avoidable that impedes human self realization is called violence".[3] In fact, violence represents a situation which hinders the people in the way of self-affirmation and self –fulfillment. Explaining the nature of a violent situation, Paulo Freire, a world leader in the field of education, writes: "Any situation in which 'A' objectively exploits 'B' or hinders his pursuit of self –affirmation as a responsible person, is one of oppression. Such a situation in itself constitutes violence, even sweetened by false generosity, because it enters with man's ontological and historical vocation to be more fully human. With the establishment of a relationship of oppression, violence has already begun."[4] It prevents "from engaging in the process of enquiry. It is one of the forms of violence because by doing so he alienates him from his own decision making and reduces him to an object which amounts to killing him."[5]

Violence, however, is primarily of two kinds, one is that which is committed by an actor, a person or a group intentionally or unintentionally directly and the other is that where there is no such actor, but violence is there through some mediation. The first kind of violence is called personal or direct violence. It is also called "classical violence." The second is called structural or cultural or indirect violence.

"The violence that kills slowly built into a structure is called structural violence."[6] "There is life and perception of life but then there is no thought of murder and hence no 'carrying it out'. There is 'death as a result of' of what? Not of 'it' in the sense of 'carrying it out' but ' it' in the sense of flagrantly unjust social structure giving very much to the few and extremely little to the many."[7] "Obviously this type of violence is not personal or direct violence like theft, killing and torturing. It is indirect lying with the structure of society. The injury just takes place as an outcome of the normal operation of the structure. The subject is at most negligent, not preventing the injury from happening. But he might also be totally unaware, not connecting the structure with any injury at all."[8]

Structural violence is concerned with disproportionate distribution of social resources. Keith Webb writes: "Structural violence may be defined as damage that occurs to individuals or groups due to differential access to social resources and which is due to the normal operation of the social system."[9] According to Ted Robert Gurr, "when the structure is made in such a way that one party suffers systematically, over time and avoidably; one may talk about structural violence."[10] The unequal distributive system of structural violence is maintained by legitimizing the prevailing political or social norms or sanctified by religious belief. John Galtung has very candidly illustrated the case of structural violence and its rationalization. Suppose a landowner has acres of land. The landless has nothing but their ability to till the land. Their landowner says, "You may till my land but you have to give me 70 percent of the harvest." The landowner feels he is generous; the alternative could have been the tractor. The peasant also feels gratefulness for the alternative could have been starvation. Yet we feel that the peasant is poor because of the foully system and the landlord is generous and honorable for the same reason. To maintain the structure of this kind, something is needed. The vested interest adopts the policy of divide and rule so that the peasant may not organize themselves and revolt against the system. The reality is mythicised with the help of ideology and religion, like 'the law to Karma', 'salvation after life', 'punishment by God', unreality {Mithyatva} of this world etc. Structural violence is also called cultural violence for the legitimization of it is rooted in our culture. It is rooted in our 'social ideologies' i.e 'deep culture', 'deep structure', 'deep ideologies' and the unquestioned aspects of culture and structure found in civilization.

To sum up, structural violence is unseen aspects of violence emanating from different structures of society, i.e. social, political, economic, educational, cultural or civilizational and it appears in the society in the forms of poverty, exploitation, domination, inequality, social conflict, 'culture of silence', social injustice, suppression and alienation. Structural nonviolence therefore needs a society where there is no poverty, no exploitation, no disparity in the distribution of necessities of life, no social tension, no marginalization, 'no rape of the Earth'. Positively speaking, such a society is guided by the principles of love, co-operation, all round justice, 'conscietization', democratization, interdependence and all-round harmony-the harmony of nature, among different castes, creeds, ethnic groups and nations, and harmony with the urges of soul. This is in a real sense a Sarvodaya society.

Gandhi's Perception of Structural Violence

Mahatma Gandhi believed in the Christian concept to hate evil and not the evil-doers. The reason behind this perhaps is that evils done by the people are not fundamental. They are the by-product of social structure. Therefore he hated capitalism, not the capitalist; racialism not the white English men and women; untouchability not the untouchables; modern civilization not the western people living in it. He very clearly saw the evil or violence present in the social structure itself.

Violent Economic Structure

Modern economics and economic systems contain in themselves the seed of violence. They have no room for morality and equality and therefore are sinful and exploitative. Gandhi said: "Economics that hurt the moral well-being of an individual or a nation are immoral and therefore sinful. Thus the economics that permits one country to prey upon another is immoral."[11]True economics cannot ignore or be the guiding disregard moral and human considerations. Therefore the foremost task of making modern economics nonviolent is introduction of moral values in regulating international and national commerce. From a practical point of view, a nonviolent economic world order should be such as none under it should suffer from want of food and clothing. Everyone should get sufficient work to enable him or her to fulfill the necessities of life. But this can be possible only when "the means of production of the elementary necessaries of life remain under the control of the masses."[12]They are also the subject of monopoly. Their "Monopolization by any country, nation or group of persons would be unjust."[13] According to Gandhi, "the neglect of this principle is the cause of the destitution of India and other parts of the world."[14] Gandhi perceives some 'disturbing factor' in the economic principles laid down by Adam Smith in his **Wealth of Nations** and that is "human element."[15]A true economics stands for social justice and Sarvodaya. Hence amassing wealth alone cannot be the guiding principle of economics. Gandhi said: "An economics that inculcates Mammon worship and enables the strong to amass wealth at the expense of the weak is a false and dismal science. It spells death. True economics on the other hand, stands for social justice; it promotes the good of all equally including the weakest and is indispensable for decent life."[16]Adam Smith's 'pure economic motive', to Gandhi, constitutes a 'disturbing factor' which prevents the economic law from having free play. If the human factor is added in economics, the whole system of present economy will have to undergo radical change.

The mode of production, consumption and distribution as well as the labour capital relationship, in a nonviolent economic structure, will take a different shape. Production and wages will be guided by the principle of the basic needs of the people. Economic activities will not be governed by the high standards of living but by the high standard of life, simple living and high thinking. Production will be determined by social necessity not by personal benefit and gain. A limit will be fixed between a decent minimum living wage and maximum income. Emphasis will not be laid on mass production but 'production by the masses'. This will logically displace high technology and big industrial production and enthrone small scale village industries, Khadi and 'economics of cow'. The individual will certainly be the owner of his property but he will feel as a trustee and use it for the welfare of society. However, if he does not hear the appeal of reason, State is free to make legislation for the benefit of the disadvantaged who can prepare themselves for nonviolent non-coòperation.

In the present economic system we experience conflict between capital and labour. The capitalists are masters and labour servants. But in a nonviolent economy, both will be co-partners in a joint adventure, as family members take part in family economy. The capitalists will give the affection of a father and the laborers will respect them like sons. Gandhi feels that capital and labor are neither subservient nor contradictory to each other. They are independent and also interdependent. It is wrong to think that economy can be built only by capital. In the developing countries, economy should be built by utilizing the labor of the masses.

Thus centralized, urban and machine economics which we have these days, are structurally violent. They cannot deliver the goods to all and grant exploitation-free society. These are the causes of violence to nature, poverty among the masses, crimes, unemployment and lop sided development or mal development. In this economy one cannot think of the highest ideal of self-realization. They are the causes of frustration, suppression, exploitation and alienation which lead to many other kinds of violence.

Violent Politics

Gandhi envisaged violence in modern politics and political structure, for the reasons that it is bereft of religion and morality. "Politics bereft of religion are a death –trap because they kill the soul."[17] They "often have a trick of wrapping truth in veil of mystery and giving to what is temporary and unimportant preference over the permanent and deeply important."[18] "When people come into possession of political power, the inference with the freedom of the people is reduced to a minimum."[19] Therefore Gandhi said: "I look upon an increase in the power of state with the greatest fear, because although while apparently doing good by minimizing exploitation, it does the greatest harm to mankind by destroying individuality which lies at the root of all progress."[20] Describing the real state of affairs of modern politics, he opined: "Today defense of citizenship is a defense of national commerce, that is exploitation. That exploitation presupposes the use of force for imposing commerce upon an unwilling people. Nations have in a sense therefore almost become gangs of robbers, whereas they should be a peaceful combination of men and women united for the common good for mankind."[21]

Political racialism, colonialism, imperialism, aggressive nationalism and excessive reliance on armaments for national security are the different manifestations of violence in political structure of world society. Even western form of democracy is also full of violence. In his words, "Western democracy, as it functions today, is diluted Nazism or Fascism. At best it is merely a clock to hide the Nazi and the Fascist tendencies of imperialism."[22]In this form of government, there is no regard for the weakest section of society which is only possible through nonviolence. The rules of majority and suppression of minority are not in consonance with nonviolence. Racialism, according to Gandhi, is a new caste system even worse than the ancient caste system of India; for, "it shamelesslv proclaims that white civilization requires the election of legal barriers in order to protect itself against Asiatics and Africans."[23] Though unseen, "it holds the seeds of world war."[24] Apparently, it seems that imperialism, colonialism and racialism have banished, but they persist in their disguised forms of commercial colonialism and indiscriminate pressure on weaker nations preventing them from becoming a nuclear power. Washington's approach to Iraq, Pakistan and India is the glaring example of this shameless discrimination. If the big nations persist in this approach to deal with international politics, world peace will always be in danger.

"At the root of modern politics lies the unseen principle of centralization of power which", to Gandhi, "is inconsistent with a nonviolent structure of society."[25] The present structure of society is just like "a pyramid with the apex sustained by the bottom"[26] and hence exploitative in nature. A nonviolent society, Gandhi said, "will be an oceanic circle whose centre will be the individual, always ready to perish for the village, the latter ready to perish for the circle of villages, till at last the whole becomes one life composed of individuals, never aggressive in their arrogance but ever humble, sharing the majesty of the oceaning circle of which they are integral units. Therefore the outermost circumference will not wield power to crush the inner circle but will give strength to all within and derive its own strength from it."[27] In a nonviolent society, "the last is equal to the first or, in other words, no one is to be the first and none the last."[28]

According to Gandhi, the nonviolent political structure will therefore consist of village republics at the grass root level, a nonviolent state governing the least and using minimum force for the governance and finally a world federation of free and independent states based on the principle of voluntary interdependence. But the question is how to change the violent structure into a nonviolent system. Nonviolence is the only answer. Gandhi invented the nonviolent method of Satyagraha which constitutes mainly three strategies, non-cooperation, obstruction and resistance. With the application of these methods, an evil and unjust system can be changed into a just social order permanently. Gandhi also suggested unilateral disarmament by the big powers to make a war-free world. He was always aware that politics is a means and not end in itself. If people become enlightened, self-reliant and capable of living in self-discipline, there is no need for a state. But today, it has become an end in itself and the welfare of people has become secondary, resulting in 'politics of violence', 'criminalization of politics' and 'politicization of criminals'. Political power has become the means for exploitation of others, not a means of protection of the people.

Violence in Social Systems

Like economic and political systems, Gandhi could also see violence in social systems of India as well as of the world. He had the deep conviction that all societies are held together by nonviolence in the same way as the earth by the law of gravitation. But a non violent society is different from the society of today. "When society is deliberately constructed in accordance with the law of nonviolence, its structure will be different in material particulars from what it is today."[29] Gandhi could give a blueprint of such a society and said, "There will be neither paupers, nor beggars nor high nor low, neither millionaire employers, nor half-starved employees nor intoxicating drinks or drugs. There will be the same respect for women, as vouchsafed to men and the chastity and the purity of men and women will be zealously guarded, where every women except one's wife, will be treated by men of all religions, as mother or sister or daughter, according to her age, where there will be no untouchability and where there will be equal respect for all faiths. They will be all proudly, joyously and voluntarily bread labourers."[30] Needless to mention that the present –day society gives an opposite picture and is obviously violent.

Man as a social being has devised some methods of social organization but they are unfortunately not in the spirit of human solidarity. Gandhi said, "We in India have evolved caste. They in Europe have organized class. Neither has the solidarity and naturalness of a family which perhaps is a God-ordained institution. If caste has produced certain evils, class has not been productive of anything less."[31]The fact is that in comparison to class, caste is nearer to truth because it does not base itself upon destruction of wealth which is the "greatest disruptive force in the world."[32] According to Gandhi, "caste is but an extension of the principle of the family"[33] for, both are governed by blood and heredity. Even if the role of environment is accepted, it can be "conserved and developed more through caste than through class."[34] To Gandhi racialism or apartheid or colour segregation is a new edition of ancient caste system of India, "which had some redeeming features, even while it is dying. But the new civilized edition has none."[35] It is pertinent to note that Dr. B.R. Ambedker saw the root cause of untouchability in the very caste system of Hindu society. He said, "The out-caste is a by- product of the caste system. There will be outcastes as long as there are castes. Nothing can emancipate the out-caste except the destruction of the caste system."[36] However, Gandhi differed. To him, "untouchability is the product, not of the caste system but of the distinction of high and low.....The attack on untouchability is thus an attack on this high and lowness. The moment untouchability goes; the caste system itself will be purified."[37]

Whether Gandhi defended caste system or stood for its abolition is a debatable question. But it is beyond doubt that he was aware of the castes as a social reality and found violence in the notions of superiority and inferiority and practice of untouchability on the basis of caste or Verna. He was the champion of the *varnashram* system in its pure form, where there is no sense of high and low and has opportunity of changing Verna by merit and action. Verna, according to him, is no "man-made institution but the law of life universally governing the human family. Fulfillment of the law would make life livable, would spread peace and content and all clashes and conflicts, put an end to starvation and pauperization and solve the problem of population and even end disease and suffering."[38] All varnas are equal because the community depends upon their services equally. None is high and none low. They are members of the same family of society. "It is canker of superiority or inferiority that is at the root of the various ills of our time, especially class-wars and civil strife."[39] "These can be ended by observance of the law of Verna, for it ordains that every one shall fulfill the law of one's being by doing in a spirit of duty and service that to which one is borne."[40] Law of Verna had nothing to do with the caste system. Castes are the distortion of Verna. True varnashram system, said Gandhi, "satisfies the religious, social and economic needs of a community. It satisfies the religious needs because a whole community accepting the law is free to devote ample time to spiritual perfection. Observance of the law obviates social evils and entirely prevents the killing economic competition. And if it is regarded as a law laying down, not the right or the privileges of the community governed by it, but their duties, it ensures the fairest possible distribution of the wealth, though it may not be an ideal namely strictly equal distribution......When people in disregard of the law mistake duties for the privileges and try to pick and choose occupations for self- advancement, it leads to confusion of Verna and ultimate disruption of society."[41] In India, Gandhi said, the failure to follow the law of Varna was largely responsible for the economic and spiritual ruin. To him, "it is one cause of unemployment and impoverishment and it is responsible for untouchability and defections from our faith."[42]

In fact Gandhi was a practical idealist. He, in his conception of social structure, tried to synthesis hereditary and environmental factors together. On the one hand, he was fascinated with the principles of Verna—a law of universal governance— on the other hand, he wanted to retain the caste system as a social reality. But in no case, he favoured class concept. He was dead against the highness and lowness, based upon Verna, caste or class. His ideal of social organization was family. He wanted to structure society in the pattern of family- "Vasudhaiva Kutumbkam"—the idea that the whole world is a big family. In such a system, every unit of society is governed by the principle of interdependence, complimentarity, co-operation, dedication towards duty and enjoys same respect, social status and importance. He did not hate caste or class or race but castism, untouchability, racialism and the concept of superiority and inferiority in their names. A nonviolent society, while maintaining plurality, is more concerned with mutuality and harmony.

If half of his life, Gandhi dedicated his services for the political emancipation of India as well as the world, in the later half, he took up the cause of Harijan emancipation and removal of untouchability. Therefore untouchability as a social system needs some discussion.

In Hindu society, whatever may be the reason, a violent system of untouchability is sustained in the name of religion and religious books even today. Though it is wanting with the advancement of knowledge and social mobility, it still persists in some concerns of society in India as well as in the world. Gandhi called it "a curse, blot and a powerful poison of destroying

Hinduism."[43]The system of untouchability is 'impure in humanity' and against the principle of brotherhood of universal humanity. Therefore, Gandhi struggled hard against it for the "complete regeneration of humanity"[44] and "brotherhood of man –be he a Hindu, a Mussalman, a Christian, a Parsi or a Jew".[45]

"Untouchability," according to Gandhi, "is repugnant to reason and to the instinct of mercy, pity and love."[46] It is "repugnant to the sense of our humanity to consider a single human being as untouchable by birth."[47]Therefore it cannot have any religious sanction. No religion of the world permits a man to call any other man inferior to him. But on the contrary, they believe in universal brotherhood. Gandhi said, "The miserable, wretched, enslaving spirit of untouchability must have come to us when we were in the cycle of our lives at our lowest ebb."[48] Untouchability cannot be the integral part of Hinduism. How can *Ramayana,* in which an "untouchable" took Rama across the Ganga in his boat, countenance the idea of any human being 'being' untouchable? That is how Gandhi argues when he was a child. Gandhi often said that, "where there are hypocrisy, falsehood, inequality and the notion that a certain person may not be touched, Vishnu, Khuda or Rasool cannot be present."[49]When Dr B.R.Ambedkar in 1953 declared that superiority and inferiority are integral part of Hinduism, Gandhi replied, "if this doctrine of utmost superiority and utmost inferiority, descending from father to son for eternity, is an integral part of Hinduism...... then I no more want to belong to it than does Dr.Ambedkar. But there is no superiority or inferiority in the Hinduism of my conception."[50]

Thus Gandhi advocated that untouchability is not an integral part of Hinduism. It must be removed from society. But this does not need the removal of caste system as it is an outcome of a sense of inferiority and superiority, not of caste system. He remarked, "It is as wrong to destroy caste because of the outcaste, as it would be to destroy a body because of an ugly growth in it or of a crop because of the weeds. The outcasteness, in the sense we understood it, has therefore to be destroyed altogether. It is an excess to be removed if the whole system is not to perish. "Untouchability is the product, therefore, not of the caste system, but of the distinction of high and lowness."[51]

Gandhi also attacked those violent systems which were responsible for the wretched condition of women in society. Child marriage, purdah system, prostitution, devadasi system, women's illiteracy and dowry are some of the systems which are the stumbling block in the full growth of womanhood in Hindu society. These institutions are made by men for their own interests. Gandhi said, "Of all the evils for which man has made himself responsible, none is so degrading, so shocking or so brutal as his abuse of the better half of humanity, to me, the female sex, not the weaker sex."[52] According to Gandhi men and women are fundamentally one. Their souls are the same. They live the same life and have same feelings. Therefore their problems in essence are one. However, down the ages man has dominated women. This resulted in an inferiority complex in them. They accepted man's domination. However, the seers of truth recognize the equal status for women. Women are companions of men gifted with equal capacities. She has an equal right to freedom and liberty with man. But, "by seer force of vicious custom, even the most ignorant and worthless men have been enjoying superiority over women which they do not deserve and ought not to have."[53] "Man and woman should have been equally treated before law and hence women should not have suffered legal disabilities which men do not. But in *sashtras* they have not been given justice, for legislation has been mostly the handwork of men and they have not always been fair and considerate to women."[54]

Man and woman are equal but not identical. Women have some special qualities and functions in society. Therefore the system of education and profession should also be made in tune with them. Gandhi said, "In framing any scheme of women's education this cardinal truth must be constantly kept in mind. Man is supreme in the outward activities of a married couple and therefore it is in the fitness of things that he should have a greater knowledge thereof. On the other hand, home life is entirely the sphere of woman and therefore in domestic affairs, in the upbringing and education of children, women ought to have more knowledge. Not that knowledge should be divided into watertight compartments or that some branches of knowledge should be closed to anyone, but unless courses of instructions are based on a discriminating appreciation of these basic principles, the fullest life of men and women cannot be developed."[55] As regards profession, Gandhi was of the view that in an ideal condition, women should not have to earn her living and should not be assigned those works which can easily be done by man.

"Just as, on the one hand, it is wrong to keep women in ignorance and under suppression so, on the other, it is a sign of decadence and it is tyrannical to burden them with work which is ordinarily done by men."[56]

For women's emancipation, proper education and removal of inertia from them are suggested as essential measures. But proper education cannot be imparted without ban on child marriage and a true education system. The enlightened women will have to organize and learn to protest nonviolently if they are interested in changing the future of both man and woman. "When woman, freed from man's snares, rises to the full height and rebels against man's legislation and institutions designed by him, her rebellion, no doubt nonviolent, will be nonetheless effective,"[57] Gandhi remarked.

Violent Education System

The education system introduced by the British in India is violent in nature, in the sense that it has no room for character building, morality, religion and all-round growth of human personality. It is violent because it alienates the pupil from his natural surroundings and from the culture of the land. It is violent because it gives undue importance to the training of the intellect and literacy education at the cost of training of hand and heart which makes the pupil unemployed in later life having no regard for human values. It is violent because it neglects the values of physical labour for earning bread and ultimately it is violent because it relies on the development of physical force at the cost of soulforce. The method of existing education is also violent because it relies on stuffing children's mind with all kinds of information and has no place for stimulation and development of the hidden talents.

A nonviolent education is not dominating and imposing but democratic, problem-posing and life sustaining. It grants all-round freedom—economic, political, social, moral, spiritual and hence all-round development. It is basically man making education and value-oriented education. Keeping all the above in view, Gandhi introduced "new education" called basic education.

Violent Cosmology

Cosmology here means, 'deep culture', 'deep structure' and 'deep ideologies', which is the unquestioned aspects of culture and structure found in any civilization. Violent cosmology, therefore, means, "cultural violence—any element in culture meaning particularly in religion and/or ideology, that legitimizes direct and/or structural violence."[58] Therefore, there are certain civilizations which directly or indirectly support violence. According to Mahatma Gandhi, modern western civilization is the symbol of violence. People living in modern civilization make bodily welfare the object of life. This civilization neither takes note of morality nor of religion. If there is anything of morality, that is teaching of immorality. If material happiness is made whole and sole of civilization, violence will be its natural product.

True civilization means good conduct and good conduct rests on simple living and high thinking. Those who will opt this life, cannot be instrumental in direct or indirect violence. Gandhi as a true Hindu believes in the unity of life and humanity. There is only one Absolute——manifested in different creatures as well as in nature and hence the whole world is a family. This belief does not permit violence to any one friend or foe. If this cosmology is realized in our institutions and personal behaviors, there will be rare chance of violence.

CONCLUSION

Thus Gandhi was the precursor of the modern concept of structural violence. He lived and was martyred for the removal of structural violence from world society. His was the real and scientific method of social change. His importance in peace research theory is unparallel in world history. Ted Robert Gurr rightly remarks, "There is major contradiction in peace theory. That between the efforts reduce direct violence and to reduce structural violence. The bridging concept is of course non-violence. The major peace theoretician and practitioner in human history, Gandhi lived in this century—Gandhi was amazingly eclectic fighting both direct and structural violence, with both dissociative and associative methods—although usually avoiding the dissociative approach to direct violence."[59]

Notes and References

1. Johan Galtung, Buddhism: A Quest for unity and Peace (Honolulu: Dae Won Sa Budshist Temple of Hawaii, 1988) Preface, pp. vii, viii.

2. Johan Galtung, "Violence, Peace and Peace Research", Journal of Peace Research Vol. 3, 1969, pp. 168-170.

3. Johan Galtung, "The Specific Contribution of Peace Research to the Study of Violence : Typologies," in Violence and its Causes, (Paris: Unesco Publication,1981), pp. 83-96.

4. Kumud Sinha, Education: Comparative Study of Gandhi and Freire (Delhi; Commonwealth Publishers, 1995), p. 143.

5. Ibid., p. 143.

6. Johan Galtung, Buddhism: A Quest for Unity and Peace, p. 138.

7. Ibid.

8. Johan Galtung, Buddhism: A Quest for Unity and Peace, pp. 75-76.

9. Keith Webb " Sructural Violence and the Definition of conflict", in Linus Pauling, ed., World Encyclopaedia of Peace, Vol. 2, pp. 331-334.

10. Ted Robert Gurr " Peace Theory: An Intoduction", Ibid, pp. 251-259.

11. Young India, 13 October 1921.

12. Ibid., 15 November 1928.

13. Ibid., 13 October 1921.

14. Ibid.

15. Harijan, 21 September 1934.

16. Ibid., 9 October 1937.

17. Young India, 3 April 1924.

18. Ibid., 25 June 1925.

19. Homer A. Jack, ed., Wit and Wisdom of Mahatma Gandhi; p. 173.

20. N.K Bose, Selections from Gandhi (1957) p. 41.

21. Young India, 21 October 1926.

22. Harijan, 18 May 1940.

23. Ibid., 2 June 1946.

24. Ibid., 24 March 1946.

25. Ibid., 18 January 1942.

26. Ibid.,28 July 1946.

27. Ibid.

28. Ibid.

29. Ibid., 11 February 1939.

30. Ibid., 18 January 1948.

31. Young India, 29 December 1920.

32. Ibid.

33. Ibid.

34. Ibid.

35. Harijan, 2 June 1946.

36. Rajmohan Gandhi, The Good Boatman: A Portrait of Gandhi (New Delhi: Viking Penguine Books India, 1995), p. 256.

37. Ibid.

38. Harijan, 28 September 1934.

39. Ibid.

40. Ibid.

41. Ibid., 4 March 1933.

42. Young India, 24 November 1927.

43. Harijan, 20 June 1936.

44. Ibid., 25 March 1933.

45. Ibid., 16 February 1934.

46. Speeches and Writings of Mahatma Gandhi, p. 930.

47. Harijan, 20 June 1936.

48. Speeches and Writings of Mahatma Gandhi, p. 387.

49. Rajmohan Gandhi, The Great Boatman: Portrait of Gandhi, p. 236.

50. Ibid., p. 259.

51. Harijan, 11 February 1933.

52. Young India, 15 September 1921.

53. R.K Prabhu & U.R Rao, eds., The Mind of Mahatma Gandhi (Ahmedabad: Navajivan Publishing House, 1967), p. 292.

54. Ibid., p. 296.

55. M.K Gandhi, Women and Social Justice (Ahmedabad: Navjivan Publishing House, 1958), pp. 5-6.

56. The Collected Works of Mahatma Gandhi, Vol. 14, p. 31.

57. Young India, 16 April 1925.

58. Johan Galtung, Buddhism: A Quest for Unity and Peace, p. 139.

59. Ted Robert Gurr, "Peace Theory: An Introduction", p. 259.

5

Gandhian Technique of Conflict Resolution: An International Perspective

Before we dwell upon the subject for discussion, let us ask two questions -whether Gandhi stood for conflict or conflict resolution? And if for conflict, how would it be pertinent to use the expression "Gandhian Technique of Conflict Resolution"? Gandhi distinguished himself for inspiring the oppressed of world, for entering into conflicts or struggles for their emancipation. He asked the Indians living in their native land and abroad, to struggle for their freedom from the British exploitation and dominance. He inspired the Asiatics, Africans and Europeans also who were oppressed, to join the struggle for their freedom from exploitation up to death. Being a Karmyogi, he, throughout his life; struggled hard for the betterment of the downtrodden, and perhaps he strove to do so life-after. When a noted industrialist asked: "Bapu you have struggled all your life against the British. The struggle has become your habit. What will you do now since the British are gone? Will you not change your habit ?" Gandhi replied: "How can I do it at this stage of my life. I will continue to struggle and you are good enough an enemy for a life times fight". All this shows that he believed in the struggle and was never in favour of the life of recluse or withdrawal. He preferred the life of action than that of meditation.

Once, he said that if he happened to meet a personality like theBuddha, he would unhesitatingly advise him to teach the people path of action rather than that of meditation.

However, this does not dichotomise the expression "Gandhian technique of conflict resolution', for the following reasons:

1. We shall see that one of the important meanings of conflict is 'an encounter with arms'. Gandhi always opposed the armed conflicts in every field of life.

2. The nature and technique of Gandhian struggles both in the procedure and achievements, i.e. in means and ends, are such that they gradually remove the tension, conflicts and opposition and ultimately pave the way for a harmonious society and world order.

3. In international politics, war is the most important form of conflict which was opposed by Gandhiji tooth and nail. He dwelt upon the problem of war in detail and provided a moral alternative to abolish it.[1] So his method of non-violence is actually a method of conflict resolution.

4. Though committed to non-violent struggle, Gandhi never made conflict as the law of society as Karl Marx did. He always explored the methodology of a non-violent conflict resolution. Whether conflict can finally be resolved or not-

Gandhi did not involve himself in such a philosophical question. What was important for him, was to seek the answer to the question of all kinds of conflict non-violently and peacefully.

The meaning and definition of conflict resolution will make it more clear.

Meaning and Definition of Conflict Resolution

The term 'conflict resolution' means the elimination of conflict. The real meaning of the term cannot be understood without knowing the meaning of 'conflict' which is the basic element of the concept. Etymologicaly, the term 'conflict' is a composite of the term 'con' and 'fligo' which mean together and to strike' or 'to dash' respectively. Thus, conflict means a fighting or struggle for mastery. It stands for the act of an active opposition. This opposition may take place at physical level or on the level of principles, statements, arguments etc. Sometimes, we also use the expressions like 'conflict of law', Conflict of interest, 'class conflict' etc. Here 'conflict' means 'discrepancy' and 'antagonism'. All this meanings of conflict, shown above are relevant for the external realities. 'Conflict' also signifies an internal state of being. In this respect it is "an emotional state characterized by indecision restlessness, uncertainty and tension resulting from incompatible inner needs or drives of comparable intensity".[2] Thus, conflict is both physical and mental, outer and inner and of the nature of thought and action. Apart from the above meaning, the term conflict' is also used specifically for an engagement between men under arms or 'an encounter with arms'. In this sense, conflict stands for violent conflict only.

From the point of view of real life situations, a contest or conflict may broadly be classified into realistic and unrealistic according to *Lews coser.*[3] A realistic conflict is that in which groups of people are involved in a conflict for a just cause i.e.

for achieving some end. But the unrealistic conflicts are irrational or ingenuine which cannot be justified by any standard of evaluation. A realistic conflict takes place over the issues of value or procurement of those things whose supply is limited'. In this sense, conflict is a means to some end.[4] Generally, the sociologists are of the opinion that a society can not be imagined completely free from conflicts. According to Max Weber, "Conflict cannot be excluded from social life". What we call peace is "nothing else than change in the form of conflict or in the antagonists or in the objects of conflict".[5] Robin Williams opines that "neither hostility nor conflict can be completely absent in a particular situation".[6] Mahendra Kumar, a noted internationalist also holds. "The elimination of violence is neither possible because conflict cannot be eliminated from international society nor desirable because violence performs or can perform important functions in the pursuit of non-violence itself'.[7] Therefore, conflicts can only be "Controlled and channelized into the desired direction".[8]

A closer examination of the above views, however, will show that they are not logically true. If the total elimination of conflicts is not possible, the term conflict resolution will be meaningless. Secondly, Kants logic that "ought implies Canst" holds good here also. If conflict resolution is not possible, the statement that 'we should resolve conflict peacefully'-becomes meaningless. It is true, that social truths are not like mathematical truths to be demonstrated in full certainty and exactitude, and hence conflict resolution, also being a social truth, cannot be understood in terms of finality. However, as a probable truth, within certain limits, it can be said that its elimination is possible otherwise all efforts towards this will be meaningless. The argument that conflict can perform certain function in the pursuit of non-violence itself, and hence its total elimination is not desirable, is the same as to argue that flood is desirable because it performs certain good functions i.e. it makes the land fertile and floods away the poisonous snakes. Conflicts which are based on ignorance can be fully eliminated. International conflict like war can be completely eliminated. The moment big powers realise sincerely the seriousness of war, though it will take time.

Thus, 'conflict resolution' simply means the solution of the problem of conflict violently or non-violently. From this point of view, a conflict resolution may hold the following positions:

(a) An armed conflict resolved through arms,

(b) An unarmed conflict resolved through arms,

(c) An armed conflict resolved through soul-force.

(d) An unarmed, conflict resolved through the change of heart.

If war is abolished with the help of war, this conflict resolution will fall into the first category. If the conflict of the non-violent resisters are resolved with the help of guns, this resolution will fall in the second category. In the third category, armed conflict or war is resolved with the help of satyagraha or soul force and in the fourth a non-violent conflict is resolved with the help of good will and understanding. The first two categories of conflict resolution are based on the logic of tit for tat and suppression of the weak which has nowadays lost its credibility. The last two are only proper ways of conflict resolution which are non-violent and peaceful and modern researches on conflict resolution are made under the postulates of "peaceful solution of intra and inter group conflicts". In international field, conflict resolution means peaceful elimination of war and warring situations like exploitation of weak nations and armaments in international relations. Thus, conflict resolution may be defined as intra and interpersonal, or intra and inter group behaviours, preferably non-violent and peaceful for solving or controlling the possible conflicting situations.

Forms and Nature of International Conflict

Conflicts, on international plane, appear mainly in two forms one in the form of injustice of the dominating nation over the dominated and the other the conflict in the form of war among nations. As a matter of fact, the former is the cause and the latter effect. The resolution of international conflict, therefore, demands the elimination of the fundamental causes of war that "*inhere* in the social and political system of the international society itself'."[10] The structural violence - the root cause of war, must be eliminated for a lasting peace. What we call injustice or structural violence in international society, is really the exploitation of the small and weak nations by the big and powerful one. Economic exploitation, racialism; discrimination on the grounds of colour and ideology, disparity among nations in the matter of natural resources and others - are the main forms of injustices and exploitations found in the international society. According to Gandhi, personal greed of the nations, their attitude of exploitation to others racism and co-operation in the matter of military operation by the people and the military personnels are the structural causes of war. He holds: "Unless big nations shed their desire of exploitation and the spirit of violence of which war is a natural expression and atom bomb its in-evitable consequence, there is no hope for peace in the world".[11]

In his view, both the systems of totalitarian and democratic welfare states are based on the exploitation of weaker races and peoples. In 1939, he wrote in The Harijan: "The democracies, therefore, that we see at work in England,

America and France, are only so called, because they are no less based on violence than Nazi Germani, Fascist Italy or even Soviet Russia. The only difference is that the violence of the last three is much better organized than that of three democratic powers".[12] Modern states rely on machinary more than the moral powers of the people. Machinary, combined with the motivation of money and resourcefulness and at the same time to equip a nation with destructive power, is also responsible for war and international conflicts. Imperialism, colonialism and expansionism all are the expressions of the above exploitative systems. In order to have a lasting peace, Gandhi suggested a new world order based on parity between nations and relation of cooperation, good will and mutual benefit forgetting the differences of geographical boundaries taking the whole world as a family.

The other form of international conflict which is more explicit, is war among the nations. War is an armed conflict or a relation between two or more sovereign or claiming to be sovereign states, established for achieving some political objective. In international politics, it plays a very important role in modern times. According to Mahendra Kumar three things are important in international politics - national interest, conflict and power. First is the objective, second the condition and the third the means of international politics.[13] Conflict plays important role, because even co-operation itself is the result of conflict. War is a specific type of conflict which is waged when real issues are at stake. Here conflict seeks a means to some end.[14] Whatever may be the purpose of war, but it is certain that war as a method of resolving conflict has been accepted by the international society for safeguarding national and international interests. And hence, we have the concept of "just war". We shall see later that Gandhi found war as inadequate and invented a novel technique of satyagraha with civil disobedience and non-co-operation a moral equivalent to war.Last but not the least, is the conflict which arises out of the mutual suspicions among the big powers. This takes the form of the arm's race not only by the big nations but each nation capable of doing it. Most sophisticated, deadly and devastating weapons are invented day by day out of this suspicion, and so we have nuclear weapons for the self-immolation. Apart from the other adverse impact of armament on society, psychological fear of insecurity among the peoples and real later conflict among the participating nations are very important.

The above three forms of international conflicts are both independently and organically true. Independently, they form three types of conflicts, distinct from each other. The first may be regarded as condition, second effect and the third cause. If the whole sequence is taken as unity, the exploitation will be regarded as root, armament trunk and the different conflicts including war as the different branches of the same tree.

Forms of Conflict Resolution

(a) *New world order*

In order to control conflicts on global scale on permanent basis, Gandhi suggested a new world order, Pyarelal, a close associate of Mahatma Gandhi in his article "Gandhian Analysis of the causes of International Tension And War", has summerized the essential conditions of this new world order and suggested some measure to fulfil these conditions on Gandhian lines.[15] In his view, equality and independence of all nations, nationalism as stone of inter nationalism, "swadeshi as a falcrum of universalism", removal of the causes of international tensions, adoption of trusteeship as a means for the removal of inequalities and satyagraha for the removal of social injustice and a ceaseless determined struggle against the passions of selfishness, lust and greed are some of the important conditions of the new world order in which conflict can be resolved peacefully and most of the conflicts will not take place in international world. For this end in view he suggested the following measures.

1. All nations and regions must be self-sufficient in respect of all vital needs.

2. Exploitation and domination by the rich of the poor, of the masses by the classes of the village by the town and of the weaker and less advanced races and nations by the stronger and more advanced ones should be stopped.

3. Decentralized economy in true sense of the term must be adopted by the nations of the world and a system of regional autonomy on the widest scale, subject to safeguarding of certain fundamental rights to all should be ensured.

4. Finally, every nation must adopt a new culture and way of life based on the principles of self-discipline, self-restraint, bread-labour and creative satisfaction. Unrestrained self-indulgence and consumerism and a socio-economic system supporting it, is very fatal to peaceful existence of society. According to Mahendra Kumar, "Gandhi's insistence was on the creation of the kind of society in which the minimum demands of all are fulfilled. But his stress was both on fulfilment of demands and on keeping the demand within limits. He recognized the truth that men come into conflict because of their demands being unlimited and that groups of men with less demands are likely to have less conflicts. He also believed that, although unlimited demands lead to conflict, the non-satisfaction of limited demands is also an important source of conflict.[18] Therefore "if new nations

try to imitate the western standards, there is every possibility of the expansion of the areas of conflict. According to Gandhi, a nation must adopt a culture of simplicity.

Most of the conflicts of society, are the product of our wrong world view. We give excessive emphasis on the differences and the element of unity loses our sight. Influenced by the Hindu idea of unity of all living beings, Gandhi teaches the equality of all living beings and nations and wishes welfare of all. This idea of sarvodaya, if implemented in the international world, all the nations will be treated as the member of one family without any clash of interest among them and each nation will not live for herself but for all. The strong will be the servant of the weak not their masters and exploiters.[19] Nationalism will not be narrow and exclusively based on selfishness. It will be a pre-requisite and stepping stone for internationalism in which "the peoples of the different countries and cultures were organized in such a way that they were capable of acting as one being.[20] Thus conflict will be lesser if this new world view is adopted.

Replacement of War by Non-violent Method

Gandhi suggested a moral alternative to war. The international community, so far, has adapted the method of violence, physical power, i.e. as the means for resolving conflicts which *accrue due* to the clash of national interests as well as far other reasons. The achievements of science and technology have proved the futility of war, as in modern times, it means total annihilation of the world. This inadequacy of violence has raised the question how to conduct conflict without disaster and use of physical powers? We are in search of a functional alternative to war. Mahendra Kumar writes:" "The real need of our time is the realization that war is essentially a methodological problem. The solution of the problem, therefore, lies in the discovery, development and adoption of alternative sanctions and means of struggle that could be used for the furtherance of our cherished objective".[21] Gandhi's contribution lies in the fact that he dispelled the cornman place notion that lead to a belief in the unavoidability of war".[22] He applied his theory of unity and purity of means and ends in dealing with the problem of international relation also. War, as a method of struggle is a means and the object for which it is waged is the end. Even if the end of war is to get justice, according to Gandhi, it cannot be realised through the impure means of war. To get justice through war is unjust, for, if one cannot give life, how can he take it? Thus he rejects even the concept of just war as a method of resolving conflict.

In modern age concept of 'just war' is not tenable even if the peaceful methods prove ineffective, all destructive nature of war does not permit us to resort to war. Mahendra Kumar, therefore, rightly holds: "The problem of theory in international relations is not to prescribe conditions for a legitimate war but -to stress that the only alternative available *to* us is to make the peaceful methods more and more effective.[23] He argues that "just cause of war" is basically an attitude of mind that is bound in time and space. Therefore, we need to develop the thinking that nothing is wholly just or unjust.[24] "The contention that war is in the interest of peace, is fallacious. For it overlooks the fact that the suppression of force can only prevent the expression of the evil in acts, but can not remove the source of the evil itself'."[25] Gandhi held: "There is a law of Nature that a thing can be retained by the same means by which it has been acquired. A thing acquired by violence can be retained by violence alone while one acquired by truth can be retained only by truth".[26] Further, "It is inevitable law that the weapon which is responsible for victory is the only one which can preserve the fruits of victory and win more.[27] Therefore, the nuclear armament can not prevent war. In his view, "the atomic weapons might have created a temporary revulsion against war, but the world would return to violence as soon as the feeling of revulsion was over".[28] Thus, Gandhi rejects war as a method of conflict resolution and suggests a novel technique of Satyagraha based on the principle of non-violence which may legitimately be regarded as moral alternative to war for the resolution of conflicts. He holds: "I do justify entire non-violence and consider it possible in relations between man and man and nations and nations, but it is not "a resignation from all real fighting against wickedness". On the contrary the non-violence of my conception is more active and real fighting against wickedness than retaliation whose very nature is to increase wickedness. I contemplate a mental and therefore, a moral opposition to immoralities".[29]

The Gandhian technique of international conflict resolution consists in the principle of struggle without arms and, positively speaking, a fight with the help of truth, self-suffering, love, character and moral powers which is known as the 'principle of non violent resistance. The exact discription of a non-violent resister, according to Gandhi, may be seen in the following stanza of Shelleys poem "The Masque of Anarchy".[30]

Stand ye calm and resolute,
Like a forest close and mute,
With folded arms and looks,
Which are weapons of unvanquished war,
And if then the tyrants dare
Let them ride among you there
Slash, and stab and maim and hew,
What they like, that let them do.
With folded arms and steady eyes,
Look upon them as they slay,
Till their rage has died away.

However, this technique of satyagraha requires greater courage and training than it is required for a military personnel. Gandhi remarks: "To seek to win in a clash of arms would be pure bravado. Not so if in defying the might of one who would deprive me of my independence, I refuse to obey his will and perish unarmed in the attempt". Further, "To kill and be killed in fighting an enemy is comparatively speaking an act of bravery but to stand the blows of your adversaries and not to retaliate is a greater form of bravery". The technique of non-violent resistance, not only holds good for resolving the interpersonal conflicts but for the international conflicts also. To Gandhi, "It is blasphemy to say that non-violence can only be practised by individuals and never by nations which are composed of individuals".[33]

Three types of behaviours are recommended by Gandhi to a nation facing aggressive situation.[34]

1. The behaviour prescribed before invasion takes place.

2. The behaviour prescribed during invasion.

3. The behaviour prescribed during the period when the occupation of territory by the aggressor has taken place.

Aggression by any nation on others takes place due to certain motive behind it. The motive may be to fulfil certain natural compulsion or to settle some differences. In the former case Gandhi suggests the proper study of the motives of the possible aggressor and removing that motive by providing suitable alternative. In 1938, speaking about the frequent tribal raids in the North West Frontier Provinces Gandhi found the raider's motive chiefly economic i.e. the satisfaction of primary needs. Therefore, he suggested to teach them industries and thereby remove their principal motive that laid them into the raiding habit.

If the possibility of invasion is due to certain differences, Gandhi forbids to take it into law court. In his view, "We should use a variety of possible approaches dictated to us by our hearts and minds, including negotiation, conciliation, mediation, sharing of differences, co-responsibility and the co-creation of a valid and creative compromise which is a recognition of the element of truth within "The other" out there".[35] He realised that "for two disagreeing parties to go to law could often be "another form of the exhibition of brute force".[36] Because, "having recourse to judiciary as a form of the Law of Aggression rules out the chance for one to practice the Law of Love".[37] If we resolve the differences with the help of judiciary, (here the International Court of Justice) it will amount to take recourse to rear, constraint and force which will never give us justice and the conflict finally will remain unsolved. Therefore, "A theory of non-violence must lay greatest stress on negotiations as the chief peaceful means of the settlement of international disputes".[38]

Gandhi prescribed another behaviour for a nation when it is faced with an armed attack. Here, the technique consists in fighting non-violently to the last consequences without any bitterness and hatred against the invador. In 1940 Gandhi wrote in the Harijan "If the Czechs, the Poles, the Norwegians, the French and the English had all said to Hitler," you need not make your scientific preparation for destruction. We will meet your violence with non-violence. You will therefore, be able to destroy our non-violent army without tanks, battleships, and airships, "the history of Europe would have been written differently".[39] The same year in July, he appealed to every *Briton* "to accept the method of non-violence instead of that of war for the adjustment of relations between nations and other matters".[40] In this context his advice to Britain is also worth to be noted. He said, "I want you to fight Nazism without arms. I would like you to lay down the arms you *have as being useless* for saving you or humanity. You will invite Herr Hitler and Signor Mussolini to take that they *want of the countries*, you call your possessions. Let them take possession of your beautiful island, with your many beautiful buildings you will give all these, but neither your souls nor your minds. If these gentlemen choose to occupy your houses, you will vacate them, if they do *not* give free passage out, you will allow yourself; man, woman and child to be slaughtered, but you will refuse to, owe allegiance to them".[41] The same type of advice is given to Abyssinia, Czechoslovakia, China and India during Italian and German and Japanese invasions.' In 1935 he said: "If Abyssinia were non-violent, she would have no arms, would want none, she would make no appeal to the League of Nations or any other power for armed intervention. She would never give any cause for complaint. And Italy would find nothing to conquer. If Abyssinia would not offer armed resistance, nor they would give co-operation willing or forced. Italian occupation in that case would mean that of the land without its people. That however, is not Italy's object. She seeks submission of the people of that beautiful land.[42] Against Japanese aggression to China, he advised, "The Chinese would say to Japan, "bring all your machinery we present half of our population to you. But the remaining two hundred millions won't bent their knee to you". If the Chinese did that Japan would become China's slave. He argued: "If it is brave, as it is, to die to a man fighting against odds, it is braver still to refuse to fight and yet to refuse to yield to the userper. If death is a certainty, in either case, is it not nobler to die with the breast bared to the enemy without malice against him within.[44] During world war 2nd at the time of Japanese aggression to India, giving justification for non-violent resistance he said to Indian people "The underlying belief in such non-violent resistance is that, the aggressor will, in time, be mentally even physically tired of killing non-violent resisters. He will begin to search what this new force is which refuses co-operation without seeking to heart, and will probably desist from further slaughter.[45] But one can doubt its efficacy during aerial warfare and blast of atom bomb. Gandhi's reply is, "Behind the death dealing bomb there is the human hand that releases it, and behind that still is the human heart that gets the hand in motion."[46]

Gandhi denounced not only the armed struggle in the case of war, but he also denounced the help of armed force from other nation. In The Harijan he wrote: "It is clear that the small nations must either come or be ready to come under the protection of the dictators or be a constant menace to the peace of Europe. In spite of all the good will in the world England and France cannot save them. Their intervention can only mean bloodshed and destruction such as has never been seen before."[47] "If I were Czech, therefore, I would free these two nations from the obligation to defend my country. And yet I must live. I would not be a vassal to any nation or body. I must have absolute independence or perish."[48] He always advised the nation small and big to fight with their soul-force the force lying within and not to take help from the outward circumstances.

In spite of the best of the efforts, if a nation loses its territory and becomes the slave of the aggressor, Gandhi prescribes a third type of behaviour called non-cooperation. A voluntary non-cooperation with the victor will make him realize his fault and arouse his moral consciousness. At least it will not strengthen his evil designs and pride, and will cause ultimate defeat to him. According to Gandhi "Non-cooperation is not merely an ideal but also a safe and quick way to freedom for India. "I do suggest that the doctrine holds good also as between states and states".[49] This is why, he suggested Abyssinia to non-cooperate with Italy. In 1942 during the anticipated Japanese attack on India, Gandhi wrote to Meerabehn: "Remember that our altitude is that of complete non-cooperation with the Japanese army. Therefore, we may not help them in any way, nor may we profit by any dealings with him. Therefore, we can not sell any thing to them. The question of having any dealings with the Japanese does not and should not arise. They will handle nothing from Japanese hands."

Thus, Gandhian technique of international conflict resolution is a moral means to settle international disputes. It consists in resolving the differences with the help of non-violence and truth in the form of satyagraha and non-co-operation. In normal cases, it suggests the method of conciliation, negotiation, arbitration, in short direct dialogue with the opponents for resolving any type of conflicts.

Unilateralism Panacia of Disarmament

The institution of war precedes the institution of armaments and armament is psychologically based on suspicion about security of the nation. It is also deemed as the mark of real power for a nation. Though in ultimate analysis, security and power based on armaments prove to be meaningless in the present situation when every day new armed technology is invented which supercedes the previous technology. Still it is no denying the fact, that mad race of armaments and lust of military powers have generated another kind of conflict in the international community which is distinguished from war itself. Here we are not concerned with their other impacts in creating restlessness in the society. We are simply concerned with it as one of the causes of conflicts and proper way to find out its remedy. All the internationalists whether politicians or philanthropists are at one in favour of disarmament at least nuclear disarmament. But in spite of their best efforts; it has remained subject of discussion only, and has yet to become reality. Gandhi, along with other moral and religious thinkers, advocated unilateralism for resolving this type of conflict on permanent basis.

Unilateralism is a broader concept which comprehends every non-violent defence[51] as well as the renunciation of nuclear and other weapons capability. But here unilateralism can be described as "voluntary abolition of weapons in the positive sense and the voluntary decision not to acquire nuclear weapons in the negative sense. It is a part of unilateral total disarmament based mainly on moral foundations, whose chief objective is to give lead in the renunciation of the use of force."[52] Gandhi believed in unilateral total disarmament. He held: "some nations will have dare disarm herself and take large risks."[53] In his view, "peace and disarmament are not a matter of reciprocity."[54] A good thing always starts from a single person. Thoreau has rightly said: "all reform all the world over always began with one person."[55] Therefore, one nation will have to take the lead. But the question is who will start? Gandhi advised that it should be started from either of the great powers. He believed: "when real peace and Disarmament come, they will be initiated by a strong nation like America irrespective of the consent and co-operation of other nation."[56] Before world war 2nd broke out, Gandhi said to Britain: "someone has to rise in England, with the living faith to say that England, whatever happens, shall not use arms. They are a nation fully armed, and if they having the powerfully deliberately refuse to use arms, their's will be the first example of Christianity in active practice in mass scale."[57] Peace will never come until the great powers courageously decide to disarm themselves."[58]

Why did Gandhi choose the big powers to start with the unilateral disarmament? The reason is very obvious. The renunciation of arms by the big power will generate moral powers among other nation. If a small country like Turky renounces the arms, it will not exert impact on other nations. But today, Gorbachev's unilateralism is appreciated by all. If Bush Govt. adopts the same policy, it will have a good impact towards the total disarmament. Late Ramdhari Singh Dinkar, a great national poet of India rightly said that forgiveness of those snakes alone are appreciated which are poisonous "Kshama shovati us blujang ko jiske pasa garal ho". The practice of non-violence by a powerful nation not only raises her moral power but it also enhances her popularity in the world. "The level of non-violence in that nation, if that event naturally comes to pass will naturally have risen so high as to command universal respect. Her judgment will be unerring, her decisions will be firm, her capacity for heroic sacrifice will be great, and she will want to live as much for other nations as for herself."[59] And if a nation raises her moral power, she can live without armament. Gandhi said: "If Germany today changed her policy and made a determination to use her freedom not for dividing the commerce of the world but for protecting through her moral superiority the weaker races of earth, she could certainly do without armament.[60]

Unilateral disarmament alone by a powerful nation is not sufficient to raise her moral powers. Along with it, she will have to shed her other exploitative behaviours if they or any of them (great power) could shed the fear of destruction, if they disarm themselves, they will automatically help the rest to regain their sanity. But then these great powers will have to give up imperialistic ambitions and exploitation of the so called uncivilized or semicivilized nations of the earth and revise their mode of life."[61]

Thus unilateral disarmament will not only help in removing global tension due to arms race, but it will also abolish war which is caused by armament. Besides, it will provide a new order of society, economy, defence strategy and political relation. In this changed structure of society, the possibility of conflicts will be significantly reduced. According to Mahendra Kumar, "A country adopting both the negative and positive type of unilateralism is likely to leave tremendous impact on other countries and these make a significant contribution to peace."[62]

However, to practise unilateralism is not an easy job. It requires courage, conviction and moral powers and mass education about the futility of existing notion of power and security. Even if unilateralism failed to cut much ice in the reduction of conflict, still it will be marked as the development of peace and culture in the whole of the world. Let the world be divided into gods and demons than to retain the only class of demon. The practice of unilateralism will help to grant divinity on earth.

Summary

To sum up the whole discussion, we have to make the following propositions. Apparently Gandhi seems to favour the conflict but in reality, he stands for conflict resolution as conflict in itself is not the goal of action and non-violent conflict amounts to conflict resolution. The international conflict which Gandhi wanted to resolve, may broadly be identified as structural, functional and a combination of the two. The exploitative socio-political systems giving birth to different types of international conflicts requires a total change in the global order, based on non-violence and parity supporting the interests of each one. War, in any form, is the expression of functional conflict which according to Gandhi can be resolved by the technique of satyagraha, non-co-operation, conciliation, negotiation, arbitration and co-creative activities. The invention of devastating deadly weapons and armament race, wrongly conceived as the symbol of power and security, bring suspicion in the mind of every nation and create psychological tension in global level. According to Gandhi, this can be resolved by the culture of unilateralism supported by appropriate change in the defence structure of the nations. As a matter of fact, Gandhi's prescription of moral means for the settlement of internal disputes is extended to the settlement of international disputes as well. His most significant contribution lies "In the role which non-violence as a technique of action and of resolving conflicts may play in a social and political system."[63]

References

1. *The New Webster Encyclopaedic Dictionary of the English Language* (Chicago, consolidated Book publishers) p. 177.

2. *Webster's Third New International Dictionary* (Chicago Encyclopaedia Britanica enc. Phillipines copy right 1976) Unabridged Vol. I, pp. 476-77.

3. Kumar, Mahendra; *Violence And Non-Violence in International Relations* (Delhi,Thomson Press (India) Limited Publication Division, 1975), p.158.

4. Ibid, p. 158.

5. Ibid, p. 158.

6. Ibid, p. 158.

7. Ibid, p. 49.

8. Ibid, p. 42.

9. Ibid, p. 42.

10. Ibid, p. 152.

11. Harijan, 10-11-46, p. 389.

12. Ibid vol. 7 P. 8 and also in Puri, Rashmisudha, *Gandhi on War and Peace,* (Newyork, Praeger Publishers 1987) 1st edn. p., 101

13. Kumar, Mahendra (1975) p. 166.

14. Ibid, p. 200.

15. Ibid, p. 158.

16. Mishra, R.P. and Gangal, S. C. (ed) *Gandhi And The Contemporary World* (Delhi, Chanakya Publication 1981) 1st edn. pp. 109-10.

17. Ibid,p . 110.

18. Kumar Mahendra (1975) p.164.

19. Pyarelal, *Mahatma Gandhi: The last phase* (Ahmedabad, Navajivan 1956) .198.

20. Puri, Rashmisudha (1987) p. 198.

21. Kumar, Mahendra, (1975) p. 161.

22. Ibid, p.73.

23. Ibid, pp. 145-46.

24. Ibid, p. 148.

25. Ibid, p. 149.

26. Gandhi. *Satyagraha in South Africa* (Ahmedabad, Navajivan) pp. 338-39.

29. *Young India,* 8-10-1925.

30. *Harijan,* 24-12-1938. p. 394.

31. Chaudhari, P.C. Roy; *Gandhi and International Politics* (Ahmedabad, Navajivan, 1970) 1st edn. 159.

32. Ibid, p. 161.

33. *Harijan* 12-11-38 p. 328.

34. Gamgal, S.C. "Gandhi And world order", compiled in *a Gndhi And Contemporary World* (1981) p. 167.

35. Mallac Guyde; *Seven Steps To Global, Change Gandhi's Message for Today,* (Santa Fe, New Maxico; ocean Tree Books 1987) p. 33.

36. Ibid, p. 31 37. Ibid, p. 32.

38. Kumar, Mahendra, (1975) p.172.

39. *Harijan,* 22-6-40,p. 172.

40. Ibid., 6-7-40 p. 185.
41. Ibid., 6-7-40 p. 185.
42. Ibid., 12-10-35,p. 276.
43. Ibid., 24-12-38 p. 394.
44. Ibid., 8-10-38 p. 282.
45. Ibid., Vol. 9, p. 112.
46. Gangal S.C. (etal) (1981) pp. 167-68.
47. *Harijan,* 15-10-38 pp. 290-91.
48. Ibid., 15-10-38 pp. 290-91.
49. *Yung India,* 8-10-25.
50. Gangal S.C. eta!. (1981) p. 168.
51. Kumar, Mahendra, (1925) p.182.
52. Ibid, p. 193.
53. Puri-Rashmi-Sudha; (1987) p. 217.
54. Ibid., p. 218.
55. Ibid., p. 218.
56. Ibid., p. 218 .
57. Ibid., p. 217.
58. Ibid., p. 217.
59. *Young India,* 8-10-25.
60. Ibid., 8-10-25.
61. *Harijan,* 12-11-38,p. 328.
62. Humar, Mahendra, (1975) p. 176.
63. Ibid, p. 75.

6

Clean Politics and Good Governance

Dirty politics and bad governance are the chief impediments in the proper development of a nation. The reason is obvious that a good end can never be realized by bad means. Politics is the means of national and social development. The contemporary India is badly in the grip of dirty politics and maladministration. It requires a radical change for its healthy reconstruction and clean politics and good governance are the only solutions.

Politics-Dirty Politics and Clean Politics

Politics, as Vinoba said, is a managerial concept. It is concerned with the good management of society. Some-times it means an activity of a certain type directed towards the achievement of common goals shared by a class or state or community or group or party. According to Aristotle "Politics arises in organized communities which permit the simultaneous existence of different groups which represent conflicting traditions and divergent interests within the same state."

Bernard Crick, making it more clear defined politics, "as the activity by which differing interests within a given unit of rule are conciliated by giving them a share in power in proportion to their importance to the welfare and survival of the whole community." Thus politics is a rational, moral and humanistic approach to develop the whole society for granting all round freedom to people.

Dirty Politics

However, politics today in India is politics only in name. Its contents have almost changed. Corruption, scams, scandals, rules by the criminals, protection of the criminals and open deceiving of the people are what we call politics. Knowledge has become slave of the opinions based on sectional interest. Power is centre and divide and rule is its way. Shameless lie and opportunism are its culture and misinterpretation and misapplication of the noble ideas like democracy, secularism, social justice and others are its philosophy. There is crisis in opinion and one can hardly understand the mandate of the people. Service and selfless service, the cherished goal of politics according to Mahatma Gandhi – the father of the nation, has become a concept found in the books. In real political activities, it appears only once in five years at the time of election, in the form of candidates seeking opportunity for service and asking for vote. It is ironical that service which is natural to politics seeks opportunity for gaining power. If all this is politics, it is dirty politics-an art of governing people by deceiving them. It reminds us of Antonio Salazar- a Portuguese dictator who remarked, "Politics represented all those noisy and incoherent promises, the impossible demands, the hotch potch of unfounded ideas and impractical plans, opportunism that cares neither for truth nor justice, the inglorious chase after unmerited fame, the unleashing of uncontrollable passions, the exploitation of the lowest instincts, the distortion of facts and all that feverish and sterile fuss." For rebuilding of the Indian nation we have to rise above dirty politics and have to be committed for clean politics.

The Nature of Clean Politics

Political activities are continuous processes. Therefore, it is difficult to ascertain a definite mark of good politics or clean politics desired by the people. However, some norms prescribed by Gandhi will help much to understand a clean politics.

For understanding the whole body of politics, we can divide it into two- End and Means.

End of the politics is the ideas, principles and philosophies which are to be realized by the political activities. The means is its strategies, method, programmes and the technology by which the political goal is achieved. Empirically speaking in a democratic policy all round freedom and development (in case of Gandhi) or "development as freedom" (in case of Amartya sen) is the end of politics. The means of politics is its government-democratic, autocratic, aristocratic, oligarchy socialistic, communistic etc.

A good and clean politics is that which is pure in both end and means. Development as freedom and democratic government in true sense, tentatively can be called the marks of a clean politics. In Gandhian terminology realization of truth through non-violence i.e. Satyagraha is the essence of clean politics.

For clean politics, Gandhi often used three concepts-politics as religious activity, politics as moral activity and politics as spiritual activity. These concepts are very similar yet different.

Gandhi did not find any activity of life separate from universal principle viz. Truth and hence he remarks, "politics bereft of religion is a death trap because they kill the soul." Due to this conviction, he never sacrificed principle of truth to gain a political end. He identified himself with the whole human kind which led him to enter into politics. He said- "I could not be leading a religious life unless I identified myself with the whole of mankind and I could not do unless I took part in politics." To Gandhi politics was a means of selfless service to the people which could lead him towards the realisation of moksha or liberation. Thus in a clean politics, there is a happy marriage of religion with politics. In other words politics can be purified, if politicians take it an opportunity for divine activity, a selfless social service and universal compassion.

Gandhi also viewed politics as a moral concept. He said – "Politics without morality is a thing to be avoided." In the whole of ancient Indian tradition politics was one of the very important moralities. It was regarded as dharma – a form of duty. Like Sadharan Dharma and Vishes Dharma, Raj dharma was also taken as a duty or moral act. Thus, in Indian tradition, politics is inseparably related with morality. To Gandhi religion and morality are the two sides of the same coin and hence there is no difference between religious morality and moral religion. His was the ethical religion. If the political activities are taken to be a moral activity, and they are performed with sense of duty, politics as a whole will be purified.

Religion and morality are the values which help us in realizing the soul or spiritual realization. Gandhi, who was very much influenced by Gokhale, felt that selfless social service was the best way of self realization. His non-violence, also called dynamic compassion, was the means of realization of the identity of souls. His political activities were also the means of self-purification. He sacrificed power in politics. In the twilight of his life, he advised the national congress to become people's servants – lokasewaka and go to the villages for realizing social, economic and cultural freedoms of the people. Thus, politics to make itself clean has to go through the spiritualizing processes. At least some enlightened politicians must sacrifice power politics and purify politics by the selfless service to the people not to the party – like Gandhi, Vinoba and Jayprakash. This will lead India to a strong democratic republic.

Clean politics alone is not sufficient for national reconstruction. It can provide only a good background for administration as the real work of the nation building depends upon good governance. Generally it is seen that due to dirty politics day to day administrative works suffer badly. Undue interference of the politicians makes rule of law a mockery. In a clean politics bureaucracy works fearlessly and impartially and people's interests are safeguarded. In fact we need clean politics for healthy public opinion, general welfare and the good governance. Let us discuss first concept of governance before we come to good governance.

Concept of Governance

The concept of governance is different from politics, state, government and regime. It integrates a number of elements and principles of good governance. Governance has been defined as "one in which the concerned authority, if any, exercises power, exerts influence and manages the country's social as well as economic resources leading to better development." According to World Bank Document 1992 governance means, "the manner in which power is exercised in the management of a country's economic and social resources for development". Governance includes three elements (a) the form of political regime (b) the processes by which the authority is exercised in the management of the country's economic and social resources and (c) the capacity of government to design, formulate and implement policies and in general to discharge government functions. "It includes the mechanism, processes and institutions, through which the national and individual groups are able to communicate their interests, make use of their constitutional and legal rights, besides meeting their obligations and mediating their differences." Broadly speaking governance is a decision making process and the process of their implementation or non-implementation. It is actually "a set of values, policies and institutions through which the society manages economic, political as well as social processes at different levels on the basis of interaction among the government civil society and private sector".

The goal of governance is sustainable development. According to U.N.D.P. Policy document, "the goal of government initiatives should be to develop capacities that are needed to realize development that gives priority to the poor, advances women, sustains the environment and creates needed opportunities for employment and other livelihood." In brief governance involves values, policies, institutions and processes of decision making for managing social, economic and political resources with a view to sustainable development. Governance may be good and bad. Only good governance helps us in nation building.

Concept of Good Governance

The concept of good governance, for the first time, appeared in 1989 in a World Bank Report on sub-Saharan Africa, Which defined the concept as "a public service that is efficient, a judicial system that is reliable and an administration that is accountable to the public". Making the concept more specific, it defined good governance, as "The one epitomized by predictable, open and enlightened policy making, a bureaucracy imbued with a professional ethos acting in furtherance of the public good, the rule of law, transparent processes and a strong civil society participating in public affairs". One of the aspects of good governance, according to World Bank is "a sound administrative system leading to efficiency and effectiveness in a democratic frame-work".

Emphasising on the organizational effectiveness, John Healey and Mark Robinson gave a picture of good government. According to them- a good government is "a high level of organizational effectiveness in relation to policy- formulation and the policies actually pursued, especially in the conduct of economic policy and its contribution to growth, stability and popular welfare. Good government also implies accountability, transparency, participation, openness and the rule of law".

Kenneth Stowe, an experienced British administrator in 1992 laid out six characteristics of good governance.

They are as follows

1. Political freedom including free speech and a freely elected parliament, assembly or legislature.

2. Constitutional and judicial protection for rights of the individual.

3. The maintenance of the rule of law by an independent judiciary.

4. The maintenance of a stable currency the essential underpinning of economic and social development.

5. Development of society as a whole by education and health care.

6. Executive accountable to a freely elected legislature.

We also find some descriptions of the concept of good governance in Kautilya's Arthashashtra. According to Kautilya's Arthashashtra there are ten characteristics of good governance:-

1. King (in modern context rulers) must merge his individuality with duties.

2. Civil servants, like greedy children, need to be watched and guided but not controlled or enticed.

3. Good governance should avoid extremes without missing the goals.

4. Disciplined life with a code of conduct is to be led by ministers and king (rulers).

5. King (rulers) and public servants must be given reasonable fixed salaries and allowances.

6. Law and order should be the chief priority of governance.

7. There should be punitive measures against corrupt officials and preventive measures for wrong doers.

8. Periodically, there should be replacement of ministers by good ones.

9. Qualities of leadership, intellect, energy, good moral conduct should be the criteria for selection of public servants.

10. There should be pursuance of good governance even amidst instability.

A complete picture of good governance will remain incomplete without the picture of bad government or governance. "A poor or bad governance has been characterized by arbitrary policy making, unaccountable bureaucrates, unenforced or unjust legal systems, the abuse of executive power, a civil society unengaged in public life and widespread corruption." The existing culture of public service is the example of bad governance.

In the existing culture of civil service, of self serving individualism prevails particularly at the top level of administration. It suffers from serious disfunction processes and cumbersome centralized system of control and ineffective implementation of agreed policy. There is lack of corporate working and high level of departmentalism among the authorities. The authorities suffer from high degree of suspicion and hostility. Few authorities are seriously concerned about strategic thinking about change and needs of the community. Scandals, affairs, scams and open dynastic rule in the garb of democracy at the top level of administration are the worst form of bad administration which have damaged the image of high authorities and sometimes they have shaken the faith in government and inspired outfits and outlaws.

7

Peace Education and Education for Peace

Concept of Peace Education

Western Perspective

Peace education is a modern western concept which has developed in the varying historical situations of the western society. Consequently its meanings, definitions, contents and pedagogy changed in the light of prominence of the problems realized by the western pacifists, peace scientists and the peace researchers. Here my concern is not to draw out historical sketches of the concept of peace and peace education, but to outline the different components involved in peace education of the west. The main objective is to analyse the different meanings of peace education, its relations with other family concepts, its contents and types as well as its methodology.

Concept of Peace

The meanings of peace education depend upon the meanings of peace. Peace covers all the aspects of human and non-human welfare. Negatively speaking peace means absence of war, direct and indirect violences, absence of luxurious way of life and absence of ecological imbalances. Positively it means harmonious world order and international relations, tension free society, enlightment, progress and development, egalitarian and just democratic society, cultural adequacy, ecological balance as well as simple living and high thinking. In fact all the above are the different facets of peace which are not independent of each other but interdependent and hence peace is a holistic concept. However peace is approached through several ways. The peace researchers consider peace as "a process on the political and socio – economical levels". The others believe in the change of values. Non-violence, love, social- justice, tolerance, freedom, trust, equivalence, responsibility and solidarity are some of the values which need to be strengthened to achieve the goal of holistic peace.[27] In this sense peace can be perceived in every situation that is characterized by non-violence and love and it needs "Continuous human activity".

Concept of Education

Education is a process of transforming the young people so that they can realize their potentialities and grow towards their fullness. In this process the educator also tries to set some norms and values which can guide their attitude and behaviour for becoming a responsible citizen of a country. In brief education is a means to arouse consciousness of the young people in its integrality.

Meaning and Definition of Peace Education

We are aware that the concept of peace encompasses almost all welfare for the all and education in the real sense of the term, is a means of transforming the whole personality of human beings. Naturally both are very intimately connected with each other. This is the reason that Mitsuo Okamoto hardly finds any distinction between education as such and peace education. He opines, "Peace education means any education which tackles the problem of violence. If one accepts this premise, one can hardly find education which is not peace education."

The purpose of education, in wider sense, is to deliver peace to the people. Thus he defined, "Peace education is a critical conscientization and self transformation of our-selves as the microcosm of the large- scale violence in the world today." However this definition and approach to peace education is tenable only with the negative concept of peace and we have seen that peace is both negative and positive concept. The author himself has discussed the four types of peace education which have not been properly accounted in his definition of peace education.

Explaining the meaning of peace education, Munfred Peters discussed three aspects of peace education. The first aspect is related with the awareness of peace related problems like security, disarmament, structures of violence and causes of conflict. The second aspect is concerned with changing participants behaviour. With the help of games and exercises they try to discover the positive sides of themselves and the others and they learn how to solve conflict without resorting to violence. In this respect peace education means educating ability to live in peace. Alexander Gross writes, "Peace education is not only a demand on external factors (other groups, society, politics) but also a demand on individuals in their personal and direct relationships within their families, in groups, in their personal surroundings." The third aspect of peace education is concerned with some pedagogy, particularly developed by Paulo Freire. To develop ability to live in peace is certainly very important thing. But the development of awareness or critical purposive consciousness is more important to discover new possibilities for a peaceful society. Paulo freire, in his Pedagogy of Peace tried to develop a method which is different from propagandistic and dominating method which make pupil naive and compel them to live in culture of silence. His concept of peace education consists of four steps of thematic universe, generative themes or words, pedagogical coding and decoding.

Thematic universe means to ascertain the range of experience. Generative words or themes mean more important theme or word in the range of experience. Today, peace is very important theme for the people of the world. The universe of peace involves so many important problems like aggression, domination, exploitation, hostility, violence, violence security, arms race, conflict, terrorism etc. These are the generative themes which need to be understood and changed. In order to do it, Freire uses two methods of coding and decoding. The pedagogical coding is laden with difficulties and requires decoding with the help of dialogue. It is different from propagandistic coding in the sense that the former has several meanings expressed in large number of data, the latter has only one fixed meaning. In the process of decoding the generative themes are recognised as problems and discussed in relation to their causes, forms and effects. Decoding is in fact a training for critical thinking.

Thus taken the above view, peace education means knowledge about peace, ability to live in peace and training to develop critical thinking about the problems of peace along with the active participation in solving this problem. For theory and practice, both form the essential parts of conscious person's determination. Dominique Pire rightly said, "To act without knowing is folly, to know without acting is cowardice".

A critical examination of the above meaning of peace education shows that peace education is training in those fields which are objectively testified. This has no concern with subjectivity. However, training in inner state of human beings is vital element in peace education. Secondly, this meaning of peace education is relevant mostly in adult education or general non-formal education. This has very little concern with value education and the education of children to make them peaceful personalities.

Lennard Vriens and Robert Aspeslagh in their article "Peace education; Alternating between the person and structures" give a more comprehensive meaning of peace education. They opine "peace education includes development of knowledge, insight and skills as well as the building up of opinions and attitude deriving from norms and values embedded in peace and directed to the realization of a human and peaceful world." This definition of peace education is based on the principle that "education is not against something, it is educating in favour of something primarily." This covers the areas of education to be imparted from early childhood to youths and to the adults simultaneously. This means that peace education has to be started from early childhood in the family and schools. In the family circle children can learn that violence is not desirable and acceptable. The author duo argue, "If the earliest educators do not make a choice for values and norms of peace, it will be very difficult to start peace education in schools and other educational institutions." This means that formation of peaceful attitude and personality begins from early childhood and hence they must be educated in values leading to peace and peaceful society. When the children grow to youth, they should be given the knowledge, insight and skills so that they can know the cause of peacefulness and also the way to peace. They should be equipped with the knowledge and informations of both local and global perspectives to raise their critical faculties and form their own attitudes to make the new reality.

According to the author-duo peace education is not exclusively the subject of education to a person or to a structure of society. It is also the education of relation between the persons and structures. For people make structures and they are also made by the structures. It means the change of values, changes the existing structures and the change of structures changes the values of individuals. Hence peace education needs both the education of peace sustaining values as well as peace promoting socio-political and economic structures, according to the stages of development of consciousness.

In this view peace education is an indirect process of revising consciousness of the people that they alone are responsible for peace. This does not give peace but directedness to education. Therefore, peace education is relevant and feasible so long there is violence and peacelessness in society. The special feature of peace education is that it works on both the educator and educatee. While educating the parents, educators become conscious of their own behaviour and attitude, orienting to peace education. Peace education, being learning through discovery, helps both educator and educatee in knowing the reality and acting according to it.

The definition of Vriens and Speslagh represents all the trends of peace education prevalent in the West. It includes in itself all the trends of individualists, structuralists and pedagogists. According to them, "the best description of peace education has to be focussed both on the personal individual who has to be educated and on the structure which influence education profoundly". They hold that peace is not only a notion playing a role on the different levels of human life and in society but it has also to be filled in several ways. The polemological approach inclines to stress the political and socio- economic structures almost exclusively. But "a positive notion of peace however is emphasizing a number of values on which a human society should be based." The cardinal values of peace are non-violence and social justice which take their shape through different values like tolerance, freedom and trust and again through values like equivalence, responsibility and solidarity. Non-violence and social justice go together. In their opinion peace can be perceived at every situation again and again characterized by non-violence and social justice and therefore it is a continuous human activity.

From the foregoing discussion, it is obvious that in the west peace is an empirical concept regarding individual, society and values. It does not take note of spiritualistic aspect involved in peace. In Indian culture peace is regarded as the basic quality of soul which needs certain spiritual training through different types of yogas to realize it. Spiritual peace is the formal action of all types of empirical peace. Therefore, peace education must include spiritual training in its curriculum.

In order to make the meaning of peace education more clear, we must try to understand it in relation of its similar concepts which belong to the same family.

Peace Education and Education for Peace

Peace education and education for peace are two different concepts. Peace education is education about peace in its different dimensions. Education about the causes and consequences of war, violence including personal violence and structural violence, values promoting to peace etc. are the main contents of peace education, while education for peace stresses on the method of education helpful in realizing peace. Paulo freire's dialogical method of education and Gandhi's Basic education and method of coherence are the fine examples of education for peace. It means that the object of peace education is peace itself but the education for peace is a quest of education and method of imparting education, leading pupil towards a peaceful life. Both concepts are similar in the sense that they revolve round the peace. But they are different in their orientations. In a wider sense education for peace is part of peace education but not vice-versa. Hence the relation between the two is not relation of identity but the relation of part and whole.

Peace Education and Peace Research

Peace education and peace research are not identical, though very closely related with each other. Peace research is actually discovery in the matter of peace. Hence it is a scientific and theoretical enquiry. But the peace education is an instrument of changing human behaviour, personality and social structure for realising the goal of peace. The polemologists specially enquire about peaceful social, political and economic structures objectively. The peace educationists try to raise the theoretical awareness about peace among the people and also mould their behaviour pattern discovering a suitable method of education. Thus while peace research is objective in its activity, peace education is both subjective and objective. The nature and content of peace education is determined by the peace researches. However, peace research is not dependent upon – peace education. In fact peace research and peace education are twin brothers in the west.

Peace Education and Peace Movement

In a broader sense peace education includes peace movement, peace research, peace action and education for human rights. However in a technical sense peace education and peace movement are different concepts. Peace movements reflected through the peace action by some groups or mass of the people originate with some problems urgently needed to be solved for a peaceful world. In the West Germany peace movement started with the slogans of Europe as an area free of nuclear weapons, use of social or strictly defensive defence instead of military difference, redistribution of national budget expenditure from military to social service, no more war and no war on German soil. Green movement was also started in Germany for environmental protection. The Dutch peace movement emphasized on "freeze the nuclear weapons, unfreeze the international relations". In the Netherlands peace movement developed on the concept of defence without nuclear weapons. Thus peace actions in the West were organized against nuclear armament war, environmental degradation, exploitation of the third world countries etc and they shaped as peace movements. Freedom movement in pre-independent India shaped by satyagraha, non-co-operation and swadeshi was a peace movement. In independent India sarvodaya movement, chipko movement, Narmada valley protection movement are peace movements with different goals to realize peace in society. So peace movements are inspired by some local problems forming a part of peace.

Peace education is the education of peace as a whole. It forms both the negative and positive aspects of peace. With this difference they are very closely related with each other. Jan Massen says, "Peace education and peace action need each other, although probably peace education needs Peace action more than the reverse." Historically, it may be said that mostly peace education developed with the development of peace movements. Robert Speslagh rightly says that peace movements are important means to convert the war culture into a peace culture. However, peace movements lack global perspectives and "to ignore the diversity of contexts is to fall into the danger of domination, oppression and structural or even overt violence which we condemn in our own particular context." Peace education includes in itself both the local and global perspectives and hence on the one hand it integrates the positive aspects of peace movements, on the other it liberates itself from the negative impact of peace movements.

As we know that peace movements start to perform some actions directly. But peace education is an indirect process of changing consciousness which starts from very beginning of life. Peace movements mostly change the consciousness of the adults and help in forming opinions for peace. But it lacks to provide cultural foundation of peace among the people. Peace education is primarily concerned with cultural and value aspects of peace and hence it begins from the very childhood of human beings in society and continues to youths and adults.

Thus peace movement helps peace education through its action where as peace education helps peace movement through its systematic knowledge, skill and insight. Both are interdependent for their growth.

Peace Education and Training in Peace and Non-violence

Like peace movement, training in peace and non-violence is sectional, local and occasional. When any type of peace action is organized, training of the volunteers becomes a desideratum. Whether they are war resisters or satyagrahis or shanti sainiks, they need some sort of training in non-violence quite different from training in violence or military training. Mahatma Gandhi intended to develop some courses for the peace Brigade. Vinoba in India and Martin Luther king Junior in America also favoured training in non-violence. This makes it clear that training in peace and non-violence is included in peace education but not vice versa. Peace education is a wider concept essentially devoted to change of conscious of people in general, where as training in peace and non-violence is meant for those who are involved in certain type of peace action. However, it is debatable whether training in peace and non-violence is essential for peace action and peace movements. But it is beyond doubt that peace education and training in peace and non-violence make peace movements easy and help tremendously in the reconstruction of society.

Peace Education and Value Education

Following the foot-prints of Swami Vivekananda and Mahatma Gandhi the new education policy advocates introduction of value education in schools, colleges and universities. The value oriented education is that which gives us insight into the inner reality of human beings to make them fully human. Religion, morality and spirituality are the subjects of value education which give us direct perception of truth resulting into self-realization. Thus value education is fully involved into the psychological or inner structure of human beings for realizing their fullness. Peace education revolves round critical awareness of peacelessness found both in outer and inner structure of human beings and society. It also seeks a non-violent way to resolve all kinds of conflicts resulting into peacelessness. This entails that peace education is both subjective and objective but the value education is essentially subjective in nature. Peace education gives us knowledge of violent, social, political and economic structures along with some selected values as tolerance, co-operation and solidarity of human beings where as value education concentrates mainly on moral and spiritual values. So peace education is the whole and value education its part.

Peace regarding Spirituality and Science

Contents and Types of Peace Education

Peace education is a growing concept. It has developed with the development of peace activities and peace researches in the West. Therefore its themes and contents have developed in course of time. Taking into account all the peace activities of the West, Mitsuo Okamoto has categorized all the contents into four categories.

They are as follows:-

1. Peace education as criticism of war.
2. Peace education as liberation.
3. Peace education as a learning process.
4. Peace education as a life style movement.

Peace Education as Criticism of War

Originally 'peace' in the West meant opposition of war. After first and second world war, the pacifists realised the futility of war on humanitarian and religious grounds and advocated for peaceful relation among the international communities. This led peace education to expose the tragedy, inhumanity and meaninglessness of war and intended to strengthen that aspects of human nature, in which peace as a value is respected. For maintaining peace in the world league of nations and United Nations organisation came into existence. Julian Huxley, Aldus Huxley and Bertrend Russell in Britain and John Dewey in America promoted peace education as criticism of war in schools, colleges and universities of United States of America, Canada, England, France and Japan. War criticism, anti nuclear education, education against Atom Bomb and Hydrogen Bomb, disarmament education were some of the important themes of this type of peace education. This concept of peace education is also known as traditional concept of peace education.

Peace Education as Liberation

In the 1970's, the peace researchers felt that poverty, unequalities, malnutrition, exploitation, domination, suppression, in one term un- development of the third world countries are more dangerous for peace than war. Therefore meaning of 'peace' changed. It no longer remained limited to abolition of war, but extended to abolition of all kinds of violence especially "Structural violence" primarily found in undeveloped and developing countries. Positively speaking they meant by 'peace' socio-political and economic structure of society guaranteeing secured life, prosperity, welfare and human rights to all without any discrimination. John Galtung, in his article "Problemeder Friedenserzieluing" (Problems of peace Education) includes a broad approach in peace education which is based on the following principles:-

1. The ruling elites determine the educational goals in order to protect the existing system and hence, education is a reproductory process of existing society which is a culture of violence.

2. Peace education can only be feasible in relation to peace research and peace action and vice-versa.

3. The Educational form has to be considered first before the content. The form does not depend upon the content

but it has its own values. The form has to be put under the light of the criterion of structural violence which is one sided communication expressing an unequal relationship. In peace education we have to act against structural violence.

Galtung has mentioned nine different forms of teaching in peace education. He emphasizes that trinity of education, research and action, is decisive for the object of peace education.

Peace education as liberation is actually a process of transformation of violent or unjust social structures into non-violent and just social structures. Here peace becomes a structural phenomenon. War is perceived as an inter relationship between violence, social injustice and underdevelopment caused by unjust structures. Peace is the absence of violence and the presence of just structure. The function of peace education is to give pupils/students insight into structures which prevent positive peace. It gives insight in their own position within the existing unpeaceful structures and also insight in the influence of these structures on their own behaviour. Thus, this type of peace education stresses on developing knowledge and insight in the big conflicts and contradiction in the world. It also helps to learn to take a deliberate view point concerning these conflicts and contradictions and the proper ways to resolve them. Finally, its goal is also to make us realize the role and involvement in the formation of these conflicts as well as in the eradication of them.

Education for the oppressed, human rights education, development education, education for justice, education for liberation, environmental education, education against discrimination, global education, international and world order education are some of the themes of this type of peace education. In the Netherlands Projects for peace Education, world studies of the Working Party peace Education, Foundation Building

Peace, Utrecht and the Polemological institute, state university of Groningen are the institutions in which peace as a structural phenomenon has been elaborated.

The main feature of this form of peace education is that it frequently takes the form of social action for it believes that teaching only through printed materials, radio, television limited in class rooms is inadequate and impossible to grasp. Real teaching is done through practical work in living situations. For "theory and practice are the essential parts of a conscious person's determination". Dominique Pire opines, "To act without knowing is folly and to know without acting is cowardice."

Peace Education as a Learning Process

The aforesaid peace educations are in fact, education about peace which lay stress on the contents of peace education viz. war and structural violences. The third type of peace education is in reality, education for peace giving stress on learning processes in given educational environment. It does not intend to impose knowledges about peace in authoritarian way but to "nurture men and women in the qualities of tolerance, imagination, creativity, criticism and elasticity" in a democratic manner. In this form of peace education the educand, instead of learning about peace, learns how to realize peace. Here educational process becomes peace realizing process and thus education and peace become identical. Paulo freire's criticism of "Banking system of education" and introduction of "Problem posing education" is the classical example of this form of peace education.

Peace Education as Life Style Movement

The above three types of peace education rest on the beliefs that peacelessness lies in warfare or poverty or authoritarian process of learning even about peace. Thus fourth type of peace education is based on the notion that peacelessness is inherent in the modern living styles of the developed countries or so called developed society or in big technology based modern civilization itself. Warfare and war preparations are intimately connected with the phenomenon of overproduction, over-purchase, over-consumption and extravagance sustained by the exploitation and poverty of the weaker nations and society. The structural violences are also maintained for the over consumption and extravagant lives of the few smaller prosperous section of society. Therefore a sustainable peace requires a radical change in the life style of the past industrial society. This fourth type of peace education emphasizes on a life style of simple living and high thinking, humanitarian outlook, self-determination, ecological awareness and personal growth. This stresses more on quality than quantity of life. *E.F. Schumacher* of England is the champion of this type of peace education. His "small is Beautiful" is the symbol of this new life style.

Lennard Vriens and Robert speslagh reduced the above four fold classification of peace education into two from the theoretical point of view- peace education as education focused on the transformation or improvement of the individuals and peace education focused on the transformation of structures within which people act. The first represents peace education prevalent in West Germany developed in the leadership of O.F.Bollnow. As we have already discussed peace education as criticism of structural violence, therefore we shall be contended here only to throw some light on peace education as the education of improvement of individuals.

In this approach of peace education, it is confessed that education is an indirect act of man and its power is very modest. Therefore, peace education can succeed only when the politicians give the pedagogues and educators enough time. Bollnow regards peace as an opportunity for man to realize himself especially in moral respect and education has to evoke this awareness. It is moral responsibility of every individual to act collectively for peace and know the meaning of peace. The task of education is to prepare individuals for peace. The character of individuals has its subjective and objective domains. The subjective domain is constituted by the person himself by ideals aims. The objective domain is the essence of the person, independent from his self images. Acoording to Bollnow both subjective and objective domains of character should be aimed at peace. For "education of subjective without taking in account the objective is empty, education of the objective is blind. Peace education attempting to touch the deeper level of human existence has to start from common things. Therefore, the task of peace education is to prepare individuals for readiness, for regular cooperation, to make them aware that experiences of every day life are often influenced by large constructions, to overcome group rivalry in favour of universal cooperation, to give new dimension of heroism, to prevent war, to shun false romanticism and promote higher estimation of reason and to strengthen people against their badly organized super individual makes so that they do not act against other people. Thus, the main objective of peace education is to build the character of individual.

Leonard Vriens and Robert Speslagh feel the necessity to synthesize both the individualistic and structural approaches of peace education. To them, "the best description of peace education has to be focused both on the person/individual who has to be educated and on the structure which influence education profoundly". They hold that peace is not only a notion playing a role on the different levels of human life and in society but it has also to be filled in several ways. The polemological approach to peace inclines to stress the political and socio-economic structures almost exclusively. But "a positive notion of peace, however, is emphasising a number of values on which a human society, should be based." The cardinal values of peace are non-violence and social justice which take their shape through different values like tolerance, freedom, trust and again through values like equivalence responsibility and solidarity.

Non-violence and social justice go together. Thus, they hold that peace can be perceived at every situation again and again characterized by non-violence and social justice and hence peace is a continuous human activity.

Education according to the author duo is a way to help young people to grow into adulthood and to prepare them for a place and task which they will take in society. For this purpose they need knowledge, insight and skills in order to hold one's own and to contribute to society. Knowledge, insight and skill are not sufficient. They need 'directedness' which finds its expression through attitude of people and through norms and values which are at their base. Thus the decisive factor of education is the change of norms, values and formation of new attitude. "Peace education includes the development of knowledge, insight and skills as well as the building up of opinions and attitudes, deriving from norms and values imbedded in peace and directed to the realization of a human and peaceful world." From this it is obvious that peace education is not directly concerned with establishing peace, but it is an indirect method of raising the consciousness of the people that they are responsible for peace. The main concern of it is to prepare the youths for peace and this process begins from the very early childhood particularly in the domain of norms and values. If the earliest educators do not make a choice for norms and values of peace, it will be very difficult to start peace education in schools and other educational institutions. But among the older children peace education addresses itself to knowledge, insight and skills to the obstacles and supporting elements of peace. Here peace education includes a critical dimension to judge the existing norms and values from the point of view of peace.

A Plea for Introducing Peace Education in India

Society of a nation always undergo its change. Though the changes go slowly, but in course of time, society becomes radically different from its previous structure. With the change of ideals and structures, its aims and objectives are also changed. The purpose of education in any country is to fulfill the new demands and meet new challenges before the existing society. Peace all round is the new demand not only in India but in the whole world. Peace education will serve this purpose in modern world society.

India Past and Present

Peace is the essence of Indian culture. It is equated with the ultimate reality and hence every auspicious work in India begins and concludes with the recitation of peace thrice.[1] The Rigveda prays for all round peace-peace of the atmosphere, lithosphere and hydrosphere and this is also recited at the time of auspicious work.[2] According to Gita, peace is the highest form of happiness[3] and a restless mind can never have happiness.[4] Except the Charvaks every system of Indian philosophy believes in Moksha as the Summum Bonum of life which is nothing but the supreme peace itself. If peace is the highest goal of human life non-violence is the highest form of morality[5] through which one can realize the highest goal of life. It is worth to be noted that the highest goal and the highest morality are not absolute. They are dependent on lower relative steps. Without realizing smaller and structural peace and non-violence, we cannot reach at our destination. Thus in Indian culture, peace is desirable both positively (a state of happiness) and negatively (act of non-violence).

However, India never witnessed such a high degree of peace-lessness as she is facing today. Mostly, Indian families are affected by domestic violences. Loot, murder, carnage, communal-riots, social conflicts, scams, kidnapping, political violences, youth unrest are very common thing in modern society. The whole society is engulfed from structural violences of economic, social and political injustices. The urban and industrial areas are polluted. Overall pollution and ecological imbalance cause fatal deseases, greenhouse effect, shortage of water resources, drought and flood. The growing population, unemployment and illiteracy pose another threat to peace and harmony. Commercial globalization and consumerism have made people restless and over greedy. Due to the dazzling effects of western materialism, Indian youths are distancing from their own culture and tradition. In short all the evils of Western materialism are enveloping the peaceful culture of Indian society. Therefore, it is high time for India to know the adverse consequences of modern western civilization which is root cause of all round peacelessness. If she is not to lose her own identity, she must educate her youths to chanalise their energy and sentiments towards realizing those trusted values which the Indian seers have given us in legacy. Indian spiritualism is very rich in resources of peace. If education, training, studies and researches are moulded towards peace, she can contribute immensely to the welfare of humanity and world peace. In ancient time, Indian society was peaceful due to its ideological and social structure. Devotion to supreme truth, performance of duty to one's station (swadharma) and simple living and high thinking were the guiding principles of general people. They valued transcendental happiness more than mundane pleasure. The desires of wealth and sex were controlled by the principle of righteousnss as to obtain moksha or nirvana was the Summum Bonum of life. The social structure was very simple. Economic management and social integrity veered round varnavyavastha in which the Brahmin, khatriya, vaisya and sudra performed their duty according to their ability and there was no economic competition and social injustices. Agriculture and village industries were the main economic activities. The society was completely free from competition and pollution as the motive behind production was consumption, not to seek market for exorbitant profit. The Gurukul system of education was sufficient to inculcate moral and spiritual values among the pupil and make them able to live their real lives. Masses could get moral and religious education through oral system of religions discourses by the religious leaders. Thus, the society was harmonious and peaceful and free from conflicts and violences. Even if occasionally conflict occurred, it was resolved very smoothly by the village panchayat. There was joint family system in which the better life for all the members of the family irrespective of their earning capacities was insured. But in modern India, scenario is different. The outlook of people is changed. They are governed by commercial, violent and directionless media and consumerism. The world is no longer a family but a market in which self-interest and exploitation of the needy weak have become the general policy. People are concerned more in augmenting their rights forgetting their duties. This is the reason behind mass inefficiency and corruption. People are hankering after raising the standard of living. Their standard of life is at its low ebb. The social structure is radically changed. The varnashram vyavastha is shattered. It is converted in to heterogeneous caste systems, People seek advantages on caste lines and enter into caste conflicts. The modern democracy borrowed from the West has created fissures in the name of sex, caste, sect, region, class and language only to secure votes to grab power. The British education system created artificiality in life destroying moral and religious consciousness and alienated people from their indigenous culture. It has created class consciousness on the basis of economic and social status causing conflicts in society. Thus in modern Indian society individuals are restless as they feel loneliness in making their fortunes. They have become greedy due to false consciousness of insecurity. Politics is unprincipled, unable to provide stability in life. Society is full of conflicts, disharmony and overt and invert violences. Only peace education and education for peace can provide stability in life and harmony in society.

Peace Education as Instrument of Change

Education is the mightiest instrument of changing human behaviour and personality. It is also a vehicle of social change.

A violent agitating and conflicting man can be made non-violent, peaceful, co-operative and noble with the help of education. Similarly, through peace education, a violent exploitative and unjust society can be turned into a non-violent, just and peaceful society very efficiently and scientifically. The fact is that war, conflict, tensions, violence and other forms of peacelessness begin from mind and violent social structure is its *bi-product*. Hence, making up of peaceful human and social structure demand the radical change in existing thinking and approaches to life and this task will be performed by introduction of peace education.

According to Upanisad, a knowledge is that which liberates, "sa vidyaya vimuktaye". To Paulo Freire a contemporary leader in the field of education, a real education is cultural action for freedom. However, the noble idea of liberating education can never be actualized unless the education is made a cultural action for peace all around and holistic peace. Peace is the fundamental need not only of human life but of the whole creation. It is basic to the growth of human personality and all round development. Therefore, the planners and executives of society should make peace education a compulsory component of educational structure. As the value oriented education is indispensable to contain uninterrupted moral and spiritual degradation, so peace education is also a desideratum in the scenario of growing violences, unrest, tensions, conflicts and structural violences of unequality, exploitation and injustices.

Gandhi's Plea for Peace Education

Mahatma Gandhi the father of the nation was the champion of peace education not only for India but for the whole world. He very intensely felt the need of educating the Indian youths towards peace. He said, "If we want to eliminate communal strife and international strife, we must start with foundations pure and strong by rearing our younger generation on the education I have adumbrated" and "If India resolved to eschew violence, this system of education becomes an integral part of the discipline she has to go through". He pleaded for the education which should be imparted through non-violence and make pupil able to raise voice against racism discrimination, apartheid and devastating nuclear weapons and positively make them able to understand the unity of humankind, the requirements of social and economic justice, eradication of illiteracy and change of certain attitudes regarding work and human dignity. He pleaded for the education which helps the youths in discerning between the basic values and outdated traditions to produce civic sense, social concience and national and international commitment. To him the seed of world peace is not engrained in the temporary expedient approaches but in the holistic approach encompassing the entire philosophy and way of life. His approach to peace was holistic and therefore, it is a great inspiration for the contemporary peace scientists and peace educationists. His ideas can provide basic foundation of universal peace education.

Western Educationist's Plea for Peace Education

Not only Mahatma Gandhi alone, but a galaxy of classical, new and contemporary educationists of the West, advocate for institutionalizing peace through peace education in their own ways. The famous Czech educator-Comenius (1592-1670) who for the first time gave a direct call for the study of peace education, considered two fundamental human traits as preconditions for peace: moderation and love. Therefore he argued that education for moderation and love are necessary to obtain peace in the restless world. The idea of lasting peace determines the whole educational philosophy of Rousseau. According to him humans are peaceful by nature. They become accustomed to war only through experience of war. However human become estranged from their natural selves because of a lack of self-respect and personal pride. Through peace education, they can realise the value of self-respect and personal pride. Froebel, the follower of Pestalozzi and Rousseau believed that peace should be an important element of early childhood education. The education of young children should foster an understanding of peace and its profound significance for human existence. This will be possible only by the reinforcement of peace preparedness and a peaceful way of life. This will help in the fundamental important interaction between speaking, thinking and acting. According to Foerster (1869-1965) through education, humans could suppress their instinctive nature and strengthen their spirit-oriented nature. To Montessori, peace is an important anthropological continuum which can be unfolded and created through the educational act. According to Oestreich (1878-1959) peace can be obtained only by the re-establishment of national culture. To him, solidarity and brotherhood are real humanity. This humanity should be the outcome of a total and productive education which is peaceful in itself. Tolstoy (1828-1910) influenced by Rousseau said that a person should be educated for self-reliance, morality, brotherhood and peace instead of for brutality, ignorance, apathy and military life.

The German pedagogues like Roth, Rorhs and Von Hentig inspired by the works of O.F. Bollnow, an existentialist, originated peace education aiming at the development of individual's personality. For Bollnow (1966) security and peace is a task of education. According to him war is not act of God or divine judgment. Therefore, peace can be considered as a human task. The realization of peace is the need of the present, not of the remote future. Peace, to him, is an opportunity for man to realize himself especially in a moral respect. Education has to evoke this awareness. However, man is not only the follower of peace, but he should also be aware of his responsibility to act for peace and through that for his self estimation and preservation. This is the enormous task of peace education which touches the deeper level of human existence through regular co-operation, large construction, chanalising the spirit of heroism among the youth in preventing war, reasonable attitude to life and ethical adjustment.

Chris Bartelds also feels the need of peace education to develop the attitude of solidarity in the individuals. He writes – "one of the central aims of peace education with a global perspective in a rich industrialized country like the Netherlands, is the development of an attitude and behaviour of solidarity with people who are made victims of injustice and oppression." This statemaent of Bartelds is not only true for rich countries but developing counties also.

John Galtung, the world leader of peace science, acclaiming peace education, opines, "starting from a negative concept of peace as absence of war and violence, peace educators have now come to accept a much comprehensive and positive concept of 'structural violence' which encompasses within itself the issues like social justice, social inequality and the problems of human rights, restoration of ecological balance etc". Justifying the structural peace in peace education, Manfred Peters argues, "A hard and oppressive social structure would necessarily influence the educational system from nursery to university, for these institution socialize the pupil in accordance with the social structure. The parent-children relationship also reflects the objective cultural conditions of the surrounding social structure. The relations prevailing in the family being authoritarian, the early upbringing of any child will be authoritarian too and will in its turn assist social oppression". The oppressive society can be made peaceful through peace education as "Peace education particularly works at changing the participants behaviour; using games and exercises they try to discover the positive sides of themselves and the others and they learn how to solve conflict without resorting to violence."

Alexander Gross also argues, "Peace education is not only a demand on external factors (other groups, society, politics) but also a demand on individuals in their personal and direct relationships within their family in groups, in their personal surroundings."

It will not be out of context to mention that the western world has established the international university of peace aiming at how to surmount prejudices; human rights; cross culture learning; the ability of mastering conflicts together, non-violent action etc. Through the technique of "dialogue fraternal" annunciated by Paulo Freire, the university also studies the theoretical peace related problems like security, disarmament, structure of violence, causes of conflict and the problem of North-South relation. It is deeply concerned with developing peace education on the principles of respect of people even in the midst of differences and the respect of the truth of facts even if it seems detrimental to our purpose and political aims.

Robert Speslagh, an eminent peace educationist advocates the urgent need of peace education in the milieu of militarism and militarization affecting the behaviour of daily life and indirectly, the whole culture of world society. According to him peace education may help us in demolishing the military culture and building a sound peace structure in society by promoting both individual's personality and changing conflicting social structure. Taking into account the various concepts of peace education prevalent in the western world, he argues in favour of peace education as follows:-

1. Peace education tries to create an aversion to violence, fosters an antimilitaristic attitude and rejects war games, war toys and the depiction of violence in media.

   It traces the causes of aggression and promotes the learning of non-violent ways of minimizing it.

2. Peace education can give people the skill to handle conflicts scientifically and efficiently.

3. It can promote better understanding among divergent people and cultures.

4. It promotes the idea of world citizenship and world government.

5. It provides us a skillful way of participation of people in changing unjust social structure and helps in building a peaceful society.

Thus the advocates of peace education may differ in the content, method and nature of peace education but all of the peace scientists, activists and those who are sincerely concerned with the ideals of world peace and a peaceful society, univocally stand for introducing peace education to alleviate the problems of a materialistic society. India may develop peace education in her own way synthesizing best from the west and rich ancient Indian culture and tradition as well as the holistic approach shown by Mahatma Gandhi in modern India. Robert Speslagh rightly said, "Starting from the ideas of Gandhi and Freire, the traditions of the south can contribute to the widening and enriching of the scope of peace education." In fact, the pleas for the peace education depict the different aspects of truth involved in peace education in order to contain peacelessness of multiple forms. Therefore, a comprehensive approach to peace education is a burning need, to institutionalise it at the different stages of our educational system.

References

1. "Aum Shantih, Shantih, Shantih."

2. "Aum dyouh shantirntariksha gwam, Shantih Prithivi Shantirapah Shantiroshdhayah Shanti.

Vanaspatayah Shantirvishwe devah, Shantir Brahma Shantih sarwam gwam, Shantih Shantirewa Shantih sa ma Shantiredhi."

3. "Prasanta manasam hyenam yoginam sukhamuttamam. Upaiti Santarajasm Brahmabhutamkalpasam." (Gita 6/271)

4. "Nasti buddhiryuktasya na chayuktasya bhavna. No chabhavayatah santirsantasya kutah sukham." (Gita 2/66)

5. "Ahimsa parmodharmah." Mahabharta.

8

Gandhi and Value Education

Introduction

The education which Gandhi wanted to impart among the children in schools and the adult in society, is nothing but a congeries of values meant to develop the all round personality and finally realise God, truth and soul called self-realization. However, he was very much aware of the fact that value education is not a thing which can be given to pupil separately along with the education of other subjects. Like the idealists he was not in favour of imposing values in the mind of pupil which are or have been conceived as values by the scholars and thinkers in ready-made form. In fact, he wanted to generate value through experiment performed in natural situation with the assistance of morally and spiritually elevated teachers. He combined in his education all the good elements of Naturalism, Realism, Pragmatism and Idealism and hence is rightly called a practical idealist. Here we shall discuss first what do we actually mean by 'value'? What relation does exist between values and education. And finally which types of values Gandhi wanted to introduce through his concept of Education?

Nature of Value

What is value? is a very complicated question. Hence, the question has been answered differently by the value thinkers. Mr. Henderson defined value as "Anything which satisfies, a human want, becomes thereby a value. To say, then that our conducts are motivated by our value is another way of saying that we act to satisfy our wants".[1] Explicitly, here value means something which has capacity to fulfil our wants. But if it is value why we do distinguish a fact from a value? Is fact not capable of satisfying our needs? Is there anything in the world which is useless and have no value in any form and at any space and time? Certainly the answer will be in negative. Therefore, we have to seek other definition which may delimit the scope of value. W.H. Kilpatrick holds, "out of man's capacity for goal seeking behaviour arise his wants and efforts and out of these come in consciously chosen end (goal) and means. Because ends conflict, man is led to weigh his goals against each other. When this is done critically enough values emerge".[2] In this definition critical selection of goal is emphasised. It stresses on the moral selection of good and evil, less important and more important. Hence, value consists in the capacity of choosing and discriminating, not in the capacity of satisfying our wants. No doubt this definition goes ahead of the definition of Henderson, yet it seems to be selective than harmonizing. Values are always harmonizing, balancing, and cohesive in nature leading human beings towards greater truth, goodness and beauty. Some other hold "values are norms for living whether social or individual. No one, not even a thief or a dacoit can possibly live without values. The choice among values could be between good values or bad values. The goodness or badness of values can be adjudged only against the social acceptance".[3] It is true that value involves certain norm, but not necessarily the norm for living individual and social life. It goes ahead in the realm of spirituality also and sometimes prescribes norms of death also. Secondly, values are always good. No doubt the notion of good changes with the pace of space, time and awareness.

Thirdly, values are not always adjudged by society. The values foreseen by the greatmen like Socrates, Gandhi and Martin Luther King and many others were not adjudged by the then society, for they were too much ahead from the general social consciousness. Similarly the values realized by the mystics are also beyond evaluation by the masses of society. Therefore, in the case of eternal values, the above definition of value does not hold good. In fact values are values even if they are not conceived by the social masses.

Sri Kireet Joshi defining value writes-Values are the ultimate ends that personality seeks to embody, express and fulfil. Corresponding to each capacity, there are specific values. Our physical being seeks the value of health and strength, our vital being seeks the value of harmony and heroism; our rational faculty seeks the value of truth and universality; our moral will seek the good and the right; our aesthetic sensitivity seeks the value of beauty and joy; and our spiritual faculties seek experiences and realization inalienable fraternity, unity and oneness".[4] According to Sri Joshi, values are not derived from any system of religion and morality, of course, the systems influence them. They are autonomous and predominantly psychological in nature. He writes- "The psychological correlation between the capacities of personality and their corresponding values is often obscured by attempts that confine values exclusively to the domain of morality or by attempts to derive values and morality from the particular religion. It is true that religions prescribe values and very often they have well-knit codes of moral conduct. However, values are at the same time, so to say, autonomous and are found to be highest expressions of our psychological fulfilment. They can and do stand apart and independent of any particular code of conduct or any particular system".[5] Mr. Joshi's definition of values gives satisfactory explanation of all the elements involved in values.

1. It is completely free from onesidedness of hedonistic, pragmatic, existentialistic, realistic, idealistic, emotive and order-theory of values which give exclusive emphasis on 'satisfaction of wants', 'utility' and 'experiment', 'helpfulness to existence', 'objectivity', 'subjectivity', 'emotionally satisfying' and helpfulness in organizing society respectively. Perfection, self-realization, satisfaction, development, integrity and cohesion - all are values but not exclusively.

2. Its explanation is most comprehensive -

(a) by using the term 'embody', 'express' and 'fulfil', the definition explains all kinds of values-material, abstract and biological-psychological.

(b) by illustrating different faculties of human personality and corresponding values- it comprehends all kinds of values - physical, vital, intellectual, moral, aesthetic and spiritual which include in themselves humanistic and political values also.

3. The determining factor of values is that they should be the ultimate ends. But the ultimate ends do not necessarily mean the only ends. They simply mean that the ends should be basic and natural, not artificial. And in this sense all which correspond to satisfy the basic needs of the people are values. To me it seems, that Gandhi conceived value in the above sense, when he said that education is drawing out the best of the pupil and it is all-round development - development of body, mind, heart and soul. "Integral education, therefore, is the same as integral value education"[6] - is hundred per cent true for the Gandhian concept of values.

Value and Education

Value and education are very closely related to each other. Values are what we strive to seek in our personal and social life. Education is the means to realise them. Values satisfy our different faculties of personality and education is the means to develop these faculties. Both values and education are selective in their nature. Values are always comparative. We value 'X' more than "Y" such valuing becomes possible only when we choose between the good and the evil and between the primary and secondary. Education develops our selective power to help us in discriminating between good and bad. Both education and values depend upon our conception of man. "Values and morality of a society depend totally on the dignity and the concept of the man himself in a particular space and time"[7] values change from time to time. Similarly, the aims of educ ation are also determined according to the concept of man which varies from time to time and from philosopher to philosopher. This is why we find difference of aims in ancient and modern educational systems.

Observing the close relation between values and education, Reid remarked, "Our questions about values and education are inseparable from larger question of values in life. Values are embodied in educational practice".[8] To W.H. Kilpatrick, the professional instrument of a teacher is what is called "map of values"[9] which consists of his hopes, aims, ideals and others. Mr. Anand P. Shrivastava holds, "Good teaching crosses the rational intellectual dimension by shaping interpersonal relations between a teacher and students. It develops mutual respect and intellectual integrity. A teacher teaches humaneness by being human, truthfulness by being truthful honesty by being honest, devotion by being devoted, generousity by being generous and social good by rendering social goo".[10] Some others view that "aims are an end in themselves and values are the product".[11] Sri Kireet Joshi finds no difference between "integral value" and integral education".[12] Last but not the least education generates values and hence, itself becomes a value.

Gandhi also finds a very close link between education and values. Modern civilization which he calls satanic civilization, is the product of English education. If this has to be reverted to new civilization, education must go a radical change. To Gandhi-swarajya is our goal. To achieve this goal we need man making education - which can develop our character and help us in controlling our senses leading to self-realization. As means and ends are identical in Gandhian scheme of thought so education and values are also identical, one being the means and the other end. Here we are faced with a question - if values and education are so closely related, why do we strive for a value education? Can there be an education without values? Is it not totological to call value education or value-oriented education? All this will be clear when we explain what a value education is.

Value Education

The term 'value education' is used in a definite sense. It is used for education which can give insight into the inner reality in a holistic framework. It is religion, morality and spirituality which alone can provide the direct perception of truth. The logical consequence of this education is formation of integral personality, total development, peace and harmony. Defining value education, Dr. Sampooran Singh writes, "Education means learning to live. Life is relationship and relationship is action. Value education is to cultivate capacity for understanding relationships which is life in its wholeness.[13] It is "concerned with the cultivation of the total human being, the nurturing of the heart-minds-brain-body system".[14] According to Dr. Singh it has two functions - one to "give the capacity to be awake to the dynamics of his own mind-brain system" and the other "to train the child in various skills and disciplines, or in other words, to learn techniques to earn one's own livelihood". The first is concerned with self-knowledge and the second with vocational training i.e. spirituality and science respectively. However, the prime concern of value education is the first. Dr. Singh opines, "The primary aim of value education is to penetrate into the innermost recesses of the mind, to be aware of the inherited conditioning; to be closed to the environment and open to absolute; and to be completely free of the mental movement and thereby enter the dimension of silence. The art of living is entirely free of the psychological suffering in the midest of all relationships".[15] value education has many advantages. It has "the capacity to transform deceased mind-brain system into a healthy, natural and attentive mind". It is "non-sectarian and non-partisan".[16] It has the common concern of the entire humanity. It promotes the ideal- "think globally and[17] act locally".

To put it differently, it is "man-making education". A man making education is an antithesis of subject-oriented and mechanistic education which concentrate on gathering of informations alone. On the contrary, "Unfailing concentration and irresistible will - this twin power has to be the basis of a man-making education"[18]. Value education gives more importance on seeing the truth which is possible only with the unagitated mind. Understanding comes only when the mind is very quiet"[19]. Learning is possible only in the state of attention.

Man-making education believes in the "sound knowledge of man and his potentialities". In it, as Sri Joshi opines, "The body has to be trained to develop health, strength, plasticity, agility, grace and beauty. Emotions are to be cultivated for the growth of nobility, courage, leadership and creative action. The mind should be developed to have the power of subtle and complex intelligence, broadness of vision, quietude, intuition and mastery of authentic knowledge. But above all this, there has to be an inspiration to fathom deep and rise high in search of truth and its dynamic execution in life and action".[20] In short a man-making education is education of integral personalty; it is education for peace and development; It is education which combines aesthetics with ethics and science with spirituality. It is education not only through letters and systems but through spirit, inspiration and experimentation.

Gandhi and Value Education

Gandhi, in modern India stands for the main inspiration for value education. His concept of value education is based on the critique of modern western civilization and reassertion of ancient system of Gurukul education. The true test of modern civilization is "that people living in it make bodily welfare the object of life".[21] There is no room for religion and morality in it. Its votaries calmly state that their business is not to teach religion. Some even consider it to be a superstitious growth. Other put on the clock of religion and prate about morality". Gandhi experienced that immorality was being taught in the name of morality and civilization sought to increase bodily comforts but unfortunately failed even in doing so.[22] This civilization, according to Gandhi, is not only irreligious but make people half-mad, lacking real physical strength, courage and appreciation of solitude. In fact it is a disease, of course a disease to be self-destroyed or cured.[23]

It is true that many cruelties have been perptrated on humanity in the name of religions, but Gandhi believed that modern civilization was more harmful than religious superstitions. "Cruelties are not parts of religion... although they have been practiced in its name...But there is no end to the victims destroyed in the fire of civilization. Its deadly effect is that people come under this scorching flames believing it to be all good"[24] he remarked. Further, "civilization is like a mouse gnowing while it is soothing us. When its full effect is realized, we shall see that religious superstition is harmless compared to that of modern civilization."[25] Gandhi was of firm conviction that India had been "ground down not under the English heel, but under that of modern civilization."[26] This civilization is the natural product of English education. "By receiving English education", Gandhi said, "we have enslaved the nation. Hypocracy, tyranny, etc., have increased; English knowing Indians have not hesitated to cheat and strike terror into the people".[27] Therefore, Gandhi thought of an alternative civilization which could be durable, peaceful and could give real happiness not only to Indians but to the whole of humankind. This is the reason he thought to revived the indigenous value education to translate his idea of new civilization into reality. He said, "civilization is that mode of conduct which points out to man the path of duty. Performance of duty and observance of morality are convertible terms. To observe morality is to attain mastery over our mind and our passions".[28] In brief by "civilization", Gandhi meant "good conduct". The fundamental belief underlying this new civilization is that "A man is not necessarily happy because he is rich, or unhappy because he is poor. Happiness is largely a mental condition".[29]

The new civilization envisaged by Gandhi, demanded a new aim of education laden with social, moral, religious and spiritual values which can very appropriately be called value education or value-oriented education.

To Gandhi, primary education and higher education of British system which are based on knowledge of letters of three R's (Reading, Writing and Arithmetics) and teachings of subjects without use in life-like geography, geometry and algebra etc. have no room for character-building and religious faith and they cannot help pupil even in getting job and hence, they are not man-making. He said, "whether you take elementary education or higher education, it is not required for main thing. It does not make men of us. It does not enable us to do our duty".[30] Therefore, we must opt our ancient school system, "character building has the first place in it and that is primary education. A building erected on that foundation will last".[31] Gandhi accepts Huxley's definition of education- "That man, I think has had a liberal education who has been so trained in youth that his body is the ready servant of his will and does with ease and pleasure all the work that as a mechanism it is capable of; whose intellect is clear, cold, logic engine with all its parts of equal strength and in smooth order. Whose mind is stored with a knowledge of the fundamental truths of nature... whose passions are trained to come to heel by a vigorous will, the servant of a tender conscience... who has learnt to hate all vileness and to respect others as himself. Such a one and no other, I conceive, has had a liberal education, for he is in harmony with nature. He will make best of her and she of him"[32]. Besides, he also believes in Upanishadic dictum- "Sa Vidya Va, Vimuktye" that is, knowledge is that which liberates us. Of course, the above two definitions of education and knowledge point to two values - ethical and spiritual values - one the means and other the end. However, both the above values are pervaded in every activity and aspects of our life. Therefore it would be better to classify the values which Gandhiji wanted to impart among the pupul through education - formal or informal.

Typologies of Gandhian Values

Values have been classified in various ways. Before we discuss Gandhian typology of values, it wauld be pertinent to dwell upan some others to understand them in a camparative way.

Dr. R.P. Singh categorises values into four types—[33] scientific or secular, spiritual or moral or religious, political and aesthetic. Objectivity, rationality, integrity, impartiality and excellence in academic matters are the scientific values. Brotherhoad, tolerance, accommodation, compassion, firmness of principles and conscience are called moral/religious! spiritual values which are deemed to be socially relevant as they help in socially cohesive life and also provide solace in the adversities of the individual. Political values vary from ideology to ideology. In aristocratic set up, obedience, conformity and humility are regarded as political values whereas in democracy freedam and equality of opportunities are values. Values of art, drama, music, dance etc. are aesthetic values. From other points of view, wealth, desires, righteousness and moksha are four types of values and Moksha constitutes the values of truth goodness and beauty - all the eternal values.

According to Sampooran Singh values may be classified into - virtue, social, ethical and spiritual. Virtue is a pattern of thought - a cultivation concerning 'what should be' and may be true or false. Social values are social uniformities or facts - moral norms or ideals envisaging ideal individual and social relationships. These are historically conditioned socio- political expressions of religion and hence local, parochial, temporarily changing with the circumstances. Both virtue and social values originate due to material reasons. Ethical value, according to Dr. Singh, is independent of past and future. It perceives the fact in present directly or intuitively as it originates from the depth-dimension of man. Spiritual value is realization of pure consciousness which is the matrix of all. Clearly this typology is based on the gradation of consciousness involved in values.

Urban classifies values into two broader groups - biological and supra biological. Economic, physical and recreational values are biological while social and spiritual values are supra-biological which consist of organizational, moral, and intellectual, aesthetic and religious values. According to Dr. Ramjee Singh, value education is concerned to introduce moral, spiritual and social values only in education.[35]

Gandhian values can be typified into developmental, religious, ethical, societal and spiritual values which must have proper place in our educational system. We shall dwell upon them separately:

Developmental Values

Developmental values can be conceived of as individual and social. From individual point of view, it is a demand for integral personality of humanbeings which means the development of physical power, intellectual power, will-power, power of the heart and ultimately soul-force, taken together. Physical power which is symbol of power of hands is essential ingredient of man's existential life which makes himself sufficient without doing any harm to others. Intellectual power means to acquire capacity to understand truth in its dynamic situations discriminating it from untruth. It actually means- 'The development of scientific temper' in man and woman. it is needless to say that to have a large number of information and capacity to recollect them is no intellectual power. The method to develop intellectual power is not contemplating in isolated chamber but experimenting in the living situation of nature.[36] Will power means power to act according to knowledge. It is concerned with our good conduct and moral power, for knowledge without action has no meaning in our real life. It is moral power which makes him superior to the beasts. Power of heart is concerned with the expression of good feelings towards others, may be called sadbhavana, which can only be generated by a morally and spiritually good teacher.[37] Soul force means 'love force', 'moral force', 'truth-force' and 'spiritual force'. But actually it is self-realization and realization of oneness in creation.[38] This force does not necessarily require strong physique but strong will and pure heart. It's education also requires the service of a spiritually elevated teacher.[39]

In Gandhian scheme of thought there is no difference in the ethics of individual and society. Therefore, like an individual, a society also needs integrated development or all round development. It means material progress divorced from social, moral and spiritual progress has no meaning for a non-violent and peaceful society. It is needless to say that capitalistic, socialistic and even Nehruvian models of development are no development as they are exclusively material development and self-frustrating having no permanant base and healthy effect on society. Thus Gandhi is the champion of all-round development as a value, both for man and society which comprehends science and spirituality in itself.

Religious Value

We have seen earlier that Gandhi held religion superior to modern civilization even if it is superstitious, for its superstition is less harmful than the superstition of civilization. He saw a great value in the teaching of religion. "Life without religion", he holds "is life without principle, and life without principle is like a ship without rudder; and just as ship without a rudder will be tossed about from place to place and never reach its destination, so will a man without this religious backing".[40] Religious experience is supreme which cannot be replaced by anyone. He writes, "the central experience of life will for ever remain the relationship which man has to God and it will never be superseded or replaced by anything else".[41] Further, "India will never be Godless. Rank atheism cannot flourish in this land".[42] All this leads Gandhi to believe in the indispensability of religious instruction. He declared, "If India is not to declare spiritual bankruptcy, religious instruction of its youth must be held to be as necessary as secular instruction".[43]

However, Gandhi used the term religion in different senses. To him religion is like culture. It is faith and conduct of individuals which vary from person to person. At the same time religion means universal moral governance of the universe. In this sense it is belief in truth and non-violence. To him religion is different types of sects. Religion also means 'dharma' - duties in different situations and finally religion is relationship of man with God. Hence, I would like to quote some of his statements in this regard.

1. 'In this respect religion stands on the same footing as culture. Just as preservation of one's own culture does not mean contempt for that of others, but requires assimilation of the best that there may be in all the other cultures, even so should be the case with religion".[44]

2. "Religion is a personal matter and if we succeeded in confining it to the personal plane, all would be well in our political life".[45]

3. "I can not conceive politics divorced from religion. Indeed religion should pervade everyone of our actions. Here religion does not mean sectarianism. It means a belief in ordered moral government of the universe. This religion transcends Hinduism, Islam, Christianity, etc. It does not supersede them. It harmonizes them in reality".[46]

4. "My religion is Hinduism which, for me, is the religion of humanity and includes the best of all the religions known to me ... I am being led to my religion through truth and non-violence i.e. love in broad sense. I often describe my religion as religion of Truth".[47]

5. "All the great religions of the world, however much they may differ, are absolutely one in this fundamental that

no man or woman with an impure heart can possibly appear before the great white throne".[48]

6. "One's respective dharma towards one's self, family, nation and the world can not be divided into water tight compartments".[49]

7. "Religion is the proper ally of art. What religion teaches people, the artist brings nearer to them in form on the plastic plane.... Art has a profound similarity with religion in as much as the fundamental experience in both of them belongs to domain of man's relationships with God.... In this relationships of man to God, it is the mysterious forces which matter, not the measure texts expressed in words. There may be changes in this relationships of man to God as represented by the various and successive religions of mankind; but to quote Cardinal Newman 'one step enough for me'.[50]

The above statements show that religion is mainly concerned with the inner life of man whether it is belief in Truth or relation with God or eternal moral principles or moral compulsions which one feels. But the question is how to impart religious training specially when religion is conceived by people as particular sects? Though Gandhi due to some practical reasons did not give place for religious instruction in his wardha scheme of education and realized its difficulty specially when the burning problem before country was to maintain communal harmony gave some guidelines which are as follows:

1. Whether there is such instruction given in the school or not, grown up students must cultivate the art of self help about matters religious as about others. They may start their own class".[51]

2. "A curriculum of religious instruction should include a study of the tenets of faiths, other than one's own. For this purpose the students should be trained to cultivate the habit of understanding and appreciating the doctrines of various great religions of the world in a spirit of relevance and broadminded clearance".[52]

3. "This study of other religions besides one's own will give one a grasp of the rock-bottom unity of all religions and afford a glimpse also of that universal and absolute truth which lies beyond the dust of creeds and faiths".[53]

4. We should read only those books of other religions which are written by authority on that religion.

5. Before we read any religious book, we must go to satsang or purify mind. "If one starts studying religious books before this stage, then instead of bringing peace this study could hinder the growth".[54]

6. One should always keep in mind that "study and appreciation of other religions need not cause a weakening of that regard; it should mean extension of that regard to other religions".[55]

However, Gandhi is convinced that the best way of imparting religious instruction is "practice of religion, not by exhibiting learning".[56] An intelligent man should put his religion on practice. He opines: "only by living a saintly life can one obtain peace. This is the way to fullfilment in this world and next. A saintly life is that in which we practice truth, Ahimsa and restraint. Enjoyment of pleasures can never be one's dharma. Dharma has it's source in renunciation".[57]

Ethical values

As we have said that the ultimate goal of human life is self-realization. Religion and morality are the means of self-realization. Morality, in fact is the foundation of both religion and spirituality. Gandhi holds, "Religion divorced from morality is like "sounding brass, good only for making a noise and breaking heads".[58] "True religion and true morality are inseparably bound up with each other. Religion is morality what water is to seed that is sown in the soil".[59] "The societies spreading ethical religion or religious ethics believe in religion through morality".[60] "Considered intellectually and scientifically, religion and morality are united and should be so united".[61] "The founders of religions have also explained that morality is the basis of religion. If a foundation is removed, the superstructure falls to the ground; similarly if morality is destroyed, religion which is built on it, comes crashing down".[62] These statements make it quite clear that without the education of ethical values, there is no meaning of the education of religious values. Therefore, Gandhi emphatically said, "Truths that are common to all religions can be taught to all children".[63] The fundamental basis of religious education should be instruction in the universal essentials of religions and a training in the fundamental virtues of Truth and Ahimsa which make for purity of heart and purity of living".[64] "A rigorous practice of the fundamental virtues, therefore, must be the solid foundation of spirituality".[65] Zakir Hussain committee also laid down, "Emphasis is to be laid on the ideals of love, truth and justice, of co-operative endeavour, national solidarity and the quality and brotherhood of man. Emphasis should also be laid on lessons drawn from life showing the superiority of truth and non-violence in all its phases and its concomitant virtues, over violence and deceit".[66]

It is true that literary training and the training of the intellect have their values on our life. But without the training in character-building, they are useless. According to Swami Vivekananda, "Intellectual training without taking care of morality makes men ten times more selfish."[67] "If education were identical with information, the libraries would be the great sages in the world and encyclopaedias the Rishis".[68] To Gandhi also, "Literary training by itself adds not an inch to moral height and character building is independent of literary training".[69] "Learning without courage is like a waxen statue beautiful to look at but bound to melt at the least touch of a hot substance"[70] he remarked.

Along with teaching of fundamental virtues of Truth and non-violence and the virtue of courage, Gandhi also gives emphasis on the cultivation of virtues of non-anger, tolerance and universal brotherhood. Asked by a girl, how to overpower anger, Gandhi replied, "Instead of asking what you should do when you get angry, you should ask what you should do in order that you may not get angry. For that, we should cultivate a broadminded attitude towards all and the feeling that we are in all people and they are in us. Just as the drops of water in sea are different and yet the same, so are we in this sea of life. That being so, who should get angry with whom".[71]

Tolerance is another ethical virtue, which Gandhi wants to inculcate among the students.[72] But tolerance is "neither respect for all religions nor it is to bear with the inferiority of other's faith". According to Gandhi, "tolerance requires the same respect to be paid to others faith as we claim for our own".[73] So, tolerance does not mean respect to irreligion or making no distinction between good and bad. The simple philosophy behind tolerance is 'treat others like yourself'. "Atmavat Sarvabhuteshu". Universal brotherhood is also a value which is needed for the modern world full of violences. Gandhi wanted to promote this value from .the very beginning of a child. However, his concept of brotherhood is very extensive He said,

"Brotherhood does not mean loving or sympathizing with those, extending the hands of fellowship to those who will in return love you. That is a bargain. Brotherhood is not a mercantile affair. And my philosophy, my religion teaches me that brotherhood is not confined merely to the human species. It extends to the 'lower animals".[74] Ordinarily it seems very difficult to love our enemy. But Gandhi argues, "If all of us are God's creation, why should we fear one another or hate those who do not hold the same belief that we do? It is cowardly fear and tolerance which lead us to hate one another".[75]

Gandhi had very deep faith in their ethical values like celibacy, non-possession, self-respect, bread labour and removal of untouchability and non-satisfying of the palate. He advised the students to become real Brahmchari which means searcher after God. However, these virtues are not only spiritually good but socially good also. All of the moral virtues have their psychological or inner aspect which are the gateways of spiritual realizations and operative or outer aspect which serve the purpose of a non-violent society. Thus, they are both scientific/social and spiritual/transcendental.

Societal Values

In modern society wealth and economics in the sense of science of wealth are given more importance than any other values. The modern economists hold material progress as the only progress of society. But Gandhi said, "By real progress we mean moral progress which again is the same thing as progress of the permanent element in use".[76] If moral progress goes hand in hand with the economic progress, there is no harm. But question is - "does economic progress clash with real progress"? "Does not moral progress increase in the same proportion as material progress"? The answer to the first question is 'Yes' and to the second 'No'.[77] Gandhi categorically denies that "material advancement means moral progress". He argues that

Rome, Egypt and many other nations lost their moral progress in material affluence. Same happened to the kins of Lord Krishna. Citing his own experience he says, "In south Africa.... I observed almost invariably that greater the possession of riches, the greater was their moral turpitude. Our rich men, to say the least, did not advance the moral, struggle of passive resistance as did the poor. The rich men's sense of self-respect was not so much injured as that of the poorest".[78] He agrees with Jesus Christ that "It is easier for a camel to go through the eye of a needle than for a rich man to enter into the kingdom of God". To Gandhi, "that you cannot serve God and mommon - is an economic truth of the highest value".[79] Thus, Gandhi concludes that "possession of riches has been hindrance to real growth".[80] "'The test of orderliness in a country is not the number of millionnaires it owns, but the absence of starvation among its masses".[81] He endorses the view of eminent scientist Wallace that "In the earliest records which have come down to us from the past, we find ample indications that general ethical considerations and conceptions, the accepted standard of morality, and the conduct resulting from these were in no degree inferior to those which prevail today".[82] Illustrating the superiority of moral value to material value Gandhi writes in Hind Swaraj, "A peasant earns his bread honestly. He has ordinary knowledge of the world. He knows fairly well how he should behave towards his parents, his wife, his children and his fellow villagers. He understands and observes the rules of morality. But he cannot write his own name. What do you propose to do by giving him a knowledge of letters? Will you add an inch to his happiness? Do you wish to make him discontented with his cottage or his lot".[83]

All the above mean that in a well-ordered society, earning livelihood should be easy and natural. It should not be regarded as separate value to realise in life. Nor education should be means to provide livelihood. It should be integrated with our livelihood. The real economic value consists in investigating the law of God or Daridranarain in which we show "how to distribute wealth so that there might not be poverty".[84]

Service is perhaps the best among the social values which Gandhi envisaged. In his Autobiography he said, "service which is rendered without joy helps neither the servant nor the served. But all other pleasures and possessions pale into nothingness before service which is rendered in a spirit of joy".[85] Replying to a question of Dr. S. Radhakrishnan he said that he believed in the religion of love in the broadest sense which means all round service. In his words, "To be true to such religion one has to lose oneself in continuous and continuing service of all life. Realization of Truth is impossible without a complete merging of oneself in an identification with this limitless ocean of life",[86] because "there is no happiness on earth beyond and apart from it". Social service, according to Gandhi means, service of all departments of life. There is nothing like high and low in social service. He enterned into politics for service. He received English education also for service. In his words "My national service is part of my training for freeing my soul from the bondage of flesh. "To me political power is not an end but one of the means of ending people to better their condition in every department of life".[87] "I do desire to serve and in endeavouring to fulfil that desire, I make use of the education".[88] This means that every activity of man is for the service of humanity - this should be the motto of our education according to Gandhi.

Freedom is another value which is important in Gandhian education. He believes in "Sa vidya ya vimuktye" But he used the term freedom in a very comprehensive sense. His 'freedom' is not only the freedom of self or moksh but all round freedom - social, political, cultural religious etc. Freedom is basic thing for the development of personality and creativity in human beings. However, freedom can not be obtained without self-discipline and self sacrifice. Gandhi remarked, "whether you secure freedom by the use of physical force or spiritual force, i.e. through self suffering, the price to be paid must be heavy if it is to be a valuable article. Bravery and perseverance in the face of odds are as necessary, if not more, to the man of the spirit as to the man of sword. Whether we win swaraj by violent means or non-violent, we shall have to discard ease and comfort, not to speak of luxuries. Pratap reduced himself to penury for the sake of what he believed to be freedom. Prahlad delivered his body for free destruction for what he believed to be his freedom".[89] Whatever price it may have to pay, in order to preserve self-respect, cowardliness has to be abandoned and that is why Gandhi said that if I had to choose between violence and cowardliness, certainly would prefer the former. Therefore, love of freedom is a value which must be generated through education.

The greatest enemy of freedom is exploitation. To Gandhi exploitation is violence. Therefore late Dr. Sugat Das Gupta holds that 'non-violence' means 'non-exploitation'. Exploitation is a "conscious seeking of such attitudes and norms which give pride of place to several social mechanisms of doubtful values, e.g.conflict, hatred and force". Non-exploitation, therefore, is a value comprising of equality, freedom, justice, love, harmony and co-operation. In other words social-non-violence denounces all kinds of authoritarianism and dominance and announces democratic values of openness of mind and respect to all. It is a fact that exploitation and injustice are co-existent with society. But it does not mean that human beings should remain a silent spectator in the midst of injustice and exploitation. Man's rationality demands to protest it but all sorts of protests are not value. According to Gandhi only non-violent protests which are called satyagrahas are values. And the technique of satyagraha involves non-cooperation with the evil, love with the opponent, to be true to one's conscience, self-suffering and adoption of peaceful way. All these values deserve to be linked with value-education.

The highest aim of society, according to Gandhi is to realise sarvodaya. Therefore, it is the highest socio-political value. By survodaya, he means all-round development of each one and everyone. The logical necessity for realizing this value is decentralization in its complete sense of power and economy. Decentralization, non-violence and democracy go together to achieve the goal of sarvodaya.

Spiritual Value

All the values discussed so far are the means to achieve the highest goal of life i.e. self-realization, God-realization, Truth-realization or Moksha. They are the ends but the spiritual value is the ultimate value which is sought to be realized by every body. The ancient Indian philosophers opted the path of devotion, knowledge, action and mediation. Gandhi took them integrally, but emphasised on the path of action and service. He said, "self-realization, I hold to be impossible without service of and identification with the poorest". He is quite aware of the role of knowledge and mediation in self realization. He opines "Food is the nourishment for the body, whereas knowledge and mediation are sustenance to the soul".[91] However he opted for the way of service which is need of the day.

Thus, we come to the conclusion that all values of life or human values are integrated with each other. When they are separated in artificial way they lose their spirit and become a burden on the mind of the pupil. When this secret of truth is realized, conflict and peace, science and spirituality, theory and praxis knowledge and conduct and lastly individual and society, nation and international community become identical and values mingle together in a greater whole. The need of the day is to disseminate Gandhian values through Gandhian pedagogy, if we want to enter into the era of peace and prosperity.

References

1. Rai, B.C., *Theory of Education* (Lucknow, Prakashan Kendra, 1988) Revised edn., p. 125.

2. Ibid, p. 125.

3. Singh, R.P., *"Values for Education"*, Tulsi Prajna, 19 (2) 1993, p..70.

4. Joshi, Kireet, *"Value Education for Secular Society"* Tulsi Prajna, 19 (2) 1993,. p. 6.

5. Joshi, Kireet, *A Philosophy of the Role of Contemporary Teachers* (New Delhi; Indian Council of Philosophical Research, 1988) p. 21.

6. Joshi, Kireet, Tulsi Prajna 19 (2) 1993, p. 6.

7. Shrivastava, P. Anand, *"Man and His Value"* University News 31 (32) 1993, p. 1.

8. Rai, B.C., *Theory of Education,* Ibid, p. 126.

9. Ibid, p. 126.

10. Shrivastava, P. Anand, Ibid, pp. 22-23.

11. Rai, B.C., (1988) p. 126.

12. Singh, Sampooran; *Science Human Values, Value Education and Peace* (New Delhi; New Man and New World Movement), 1993, p. 39.

13. Ibid, p. 40.

14. Ibid, p. 40.

15. Ibid, p. 41.

16. Joshi, Kireet; *A Philosophy of Education for the Contemporary Youth* (New Delhi, Indian Society of Philosophical Resparch, 1985) p. 12.
17. Singh, Sampooran, (1993), p. 30.
18. Joshi, Kireet, (1985) p. 12.
19. Gandhi, M.K. *Hind Swaraj or Indian Home Rule* (Ahmedabad, Navajivan Publishing House, 1990) eighth reprint, p. 32.
20. Ibid, p. 33.
21. Ibid, p. 33.
22. Ibid, p. 34.
23. Ibid, p. 39.
24. Ibid, p. 39.
25. Ibid, p. 38.
26. Ibid, p. 80.
27. Ibid, p. 55.
28. Ibid, p. 55.
29. Ibid, p. 78.
30. Ibid, p. 79.
31. Ibid, p. 78.
32. Tulsi Prajna 19 (2) 1993, p. 71.
33. Singh, Sampooran, (1993) pp. 24-25.
34. Singh, *Dashrath, Samaj Ki Nai Disayen* (Ladnun Jain Vishva Bharati Institute, 1993) p. 34.
35. Singh, Dashrath, *Gandhi vad Iw Vinoba Ki Den* (Patna,Bihar, Hindi Granth Academy, 1975) p. 572.

36. Gandhi, M.K. *Towards New Education,* p. 22 Singh, Dashrath, (1975) p. 571.

37. Ayer, Raghavan, ed., *The Moral and Political Writings of Mahatma Gandhi* (Oxford, Clarendon Press 1986) Vol. I, p. 529.

38. (a) "A. teacher teaches humaneness by being humane, truthfulness by being truthful, honesty by being honest, devotion by being devoted, generosity by being generous and social good by rendering social good" - Anand P. Srivastava.

    (b) 'You can not effect any change in others unless you have effected the change in yourself'- Kireet Joshi.

    (c) "The best way to do this (give religious education) in my opinion is for the teachers rigorously to practise these virtues in their own person" - Gandhi.

39. Patel, M.S., The Educational Philosophy of Mahatma Gandhi (Ahamedabad, Navajivan Publishing House, 1953) p. 200.

40. Iyer, Raghavan, ed., *The Moral and Political Writings of Mahatma Gandhi,* Vol. 1, p. 459.

41. Gandhi, M.K. *Hid Swaraj or Home Rule,* Ibid, p. 67.

42 Gandhi, M.K., *Young India,* 25.8.1927.

43. Gandhi, *Young India,* 6.12.1928 & Iyer, Raghavan, ed., *The Moral and Political Writings of Mahatma Gandhi* Vol. I, p. 451.

44. Tulsi Prajn (19 (1) 1993, p. 14 & *Harijan* 31.8.1947.

45. *Harijan* 10. 2. 1940.

46. Iyer, Raghavan; *The Moral and Political Writings of Mahatma Gandhi,* Ibid, Vol. I. p. 461.

47. Patel, M.S., *The Educational Philosophy of Mahatma Gandhi,* Ibid, p. 207.

48. Iyer, Raghavan; *The Moral and Political Writings of Mahatma Gandhi,* Vol. II, p. 81.

49. Ibid, Vol. I, p. 459.

50. *Young India,* 25.8.1927.

51. Ibid, 6.12.1928.

52. Ibid.

53. Iyer, Raghavan; *The Moral and Political Writings of Mahatma Gandhi,* Vol. II, p. 76.

54. *Young India,* 6.12.1928.

55. Iyer, Raghavan; *The Moral and Political Writings of Mahatma Gandhi,* Vol. II, p. 76.

56. Ibid, p. 76.

57. Patel, M.S., *The Educational Philosophy of Mahatma Gandhi* p. 206.

58. Ibid, p. 76.

59. Narayan, Shriman, *The Selected Works. of Mahatma Gandhi* (Ahmedabad, Navajivan Publishing House, 1968), Vol. IV, p. 21.

60. Ibid, pp. 22-23.

61. Gandhi, M.K. *Education Reconstruction* CWardha, Hindustani Talimi Sangh) p. 147.

62. Patel, M.S., *The Educational Philosophy of Mahatma Gandhi,* p. 207.

63. Ibid, p. 207.

64. Ibid, p. 209.

65. *The Complete Works of Swami Vivenananda* (Mayavati: Almora 1962)Vol. I, p. 412.

66. Ibid, Vol. III, p. 302.

67. *Young India,* 1.6.1924.

68. Ibid, 12.7.1928.

69. Iyer, Raghavan; *The Moral and Political Writings of Mahatma Gandhi,* Vol. II, p. 116.

70. Ibid, Vol. I, p. 542.

71. Ibid, p. 542.

72. Ibid, p. 529.

73. Ibid, p. 530.

74. Ibid, Vol. II, p. 356.

75. Ibid, p. 357.

76. Ibid, p. 357.

77. Ibid, p. 359.

78. Ibid, p. 357.

79. Ibid, p. 357.

80. Ibid, p. 360.

81. Gandhi, M.K., *Hindi Swaraj,* p. 78.

82. Gandhi, M.K. An Autobiography (Ahmedabad, Navajivan Publishing House 1927) 2nd edn. pp. 130-31.

83. Iyer, Raghavan, *The Moral and Political Writings of Mahatma Gandhi* Vol. I, p. 461.

84. Ibid, p. 46.

85. Ibid, p. 399.

86. *Hind Swaraj,* p. 79.

87. *Young India,* 9.12.1926.

88. "Selfless Service is the Secret of Life. To rise above passions is the highest ideal".

9

Sarvodaya

Principles of Sarvodaya

'Sarvodaya' is a concept, having its deep root in Indian philosophical traditions, though, it does not mean that the western thinking, especially religious thought, are devoid of it. The concept has been used as 'good will to all' (Sarva Mangal bhavana) in both the Vedantic as well as Buddhistic traditions. 'Sarva bhavantu sukinah' (Let all be happy) of the Vedas, 'ten tykten bhungithah ma gridhah kashyaschi- ddhanam' (find your enjoyment after offering it to God) of the Upanishad, 'Sarva bhut hite ratah' (engaged in the welfare of all living beings) of the Gita, 'bahujan hitaya bahujan sukhaya' (in the interest of public good) of Lord Buddha are the expressions of noble feelings for others which glorify the values of universal friendship (Maitri), compassion (karuna), love, altruism, neutrality (upekksha) and equality (samta). For the first time, in the history of Indian Philosophy, Acharya Samantbhadra – a Jain philosopher, used the concept 'Sarvodaya Tirth' in his book, 'Yuktyanushasan'. He used the term as an adjective or the substitute for the whole of the teachings of Lord Mahavir, constituting the principles of manifoldness of reality (Anekantvad) and relativity of knowledge (syadvad), which emancipate all from suffering and lead to salvation. Here, the concept 'Sarvodaya tirth'[1] stood for 'the spiritual upliftment of all'. It had little concern with the socio-economic and other mundane welfare of the people. Its main emphasis was on universal non-violence, which includes all living beings, great or small. In advait Vedant, especially, in the philosophy of Shankaracharya, 'Sarvodaya' is not 'welfare of all' but realization of one absolute in all - that is salvation. There are sarvodaya elements in Bible, which inspired Ruskin, Tolstoy and others, but there is no ideology or principles of sarvodaya in explicit form.

It was Gandhi, in modern times, who for the first time, coined the term 'Sarvodaya' paraphrasing Ruskin's "Unto this last" in Gujarati language and evolved from it a complete ideology of Sarvodaya. As, he was assassinated in the very dawn of India's political freedom, he could not develop the principles of Sarvodaya in detail, which was fulfilled by Acharya Vinoba Bhave through his Sarvodaya movement and followed by Jayprakash Narayan and other contemporaries of Gandhi and Vinoba.

I shall try to point out certain principles of Sarvodaya ideology.

Before, we go deep into the problem; it would not be out of place to examine some of the views expressed by the eminent scholars of Gandhian ideology.

Sarvodaya a Social Movement

Generally, Sarvodaya thinkers and scholars hold 'Sarvodaya' a term signifying a social movement. Prof. K. Arunachalam writes: - "Sarvodaya is a dynamic growing social movement that is continually evolving as it confronts new situations and fresh problems". For him, the term stands for a society which is different from both capitalistic and socialistic societies.[2]

No doubt, the term Sarvodaya got its currency as a land reform, Sarvodaya movement led by Vinoba and J.P. It is also true, that the word stands for a society of which Gandhi himself gave a blue print-though incomplete. But these expressions do not comprehend some other important aspects of Sarvodaya ideology. Sarvodaya is not only a theory regarding society and social events but also a complete philosophy of life based on its own world-view as well as moral values. Further, 'society' is a very comprehensive term. It has different distinguishing elements like Politics, Economics, Education etc. Sarvodaya not only presents an ideal picture of society but it has also political, economic, educational and social theories. Moreover, Sarvodaya is not only a theory, but also a practice. If we use Paulo Freire's term, we may legitimately call it a 'Praxis'.[3]

Prof. V.K.R.V. Rao, an eminent economist of India, conceives of Sarvodaya as 'a classless society', 'a system of production', 'a system of distribution', 'a social order', 'a political system' and 'a life spent in dedication to God and spent in cultivation of spirit'.[4]

The merit of such descriptions of Sarvodaya lies in covering a wider range of its ideology. But it lacks a universal co-ordinating principle on which all theories can be organized into a systematic whole. Moreover, the above descriptions of Sarvodaya are mere descriptions of its middle part of the body. The leg and the head – the ground and the goal have been left untouched. Sarvodaya has good metaphysical ground and its has an ultimate purpose to establish world peace through a right system of education. Further, what Mr. Rao describes under 'political system', is in fact, a methodology of social change and change of human personality. As a political system, Sarvodaya stands for village democracy – where every unit of the nation will be self-sufficient both economically and politically. Last but not the least, 'Sarvodaya' is not only an adjective to be used to qualify some entities. It is an entity itself constituting different principles in it.

Thus, we find, that Prof. Rao's description of sarvodaya, does not take into account the unifying principles. So it is incomplete. It may be regarded as the applied form of Sarvodaya – not the principle underlying it.

Dr. V.P. Verma removes all the difficulties arising out of the above descriptions and holds Sarvodaya as an integral and synthetic philosophy.[5] He envisages different kinds of synthesis[6] in the ideology of Sarvodaya, with a sound spiritualistic metaphysics – though doubtful about the relevance of metaphysics for the idea of welfare of all. His leaning is towards Lord Buddha.

Sarvodaya, no doubt, is an integral and synthetic philosophy. But a synthesis in integral whole can not be possible without the help of principles. Dr. Verma also fails to evolve those principles on which synthesis is made. In absence of those principles, Sarvodaya will be mere ecleptical than synthetical. He is interested in showing what types of synthesis are there only. How and why they are so has not been discussed in the ideology of Sarvodaya.

Moreover, the relevance of spiritualistic metaphysics in Sarvodaya cannot be doubted. Philosophy of Sarvodaya is not grounded exclusively on intellectualism. It is based on the whole experience of Gandhi and Vinoba. In total experience, mysticism, faith, human psychology play very important role. India is a country of spiritualism. Any ideology devoid of this spiritualistic note cannot gain ground here. The ideology of Sarvodaya cannot be realised in practice without appealing to the mass psychology. Buddhism, though it denies metaphysics and mysticism in philosophical discussion, yet could not deny mysticism in the concept of Nirvana – a mystic state of experience. Moreover,

Buddhism, as a religion could survive only on the mystification of Lord Buddha. Therefore, the realization of Sarvodaya is neither possible on the basis of flux and void nor on the basis of materialism. It must be based on the highest truth which is spiritual in nature.

Sarvodaya, though, integral and synthetic philosophy, is not a complete and final synthesis. Nor is it a static ideology. Its synthesis is not the synthesis of contradictions, but a harmonious blending of all the noble thoughts of the East and the West.

From the review of the above view points, it appears that they give only the applied aspects of Sarvodaya. The main principles have not been touched. Here we shall deal with the main principles which underlie all the Sarvodaya movements, programmes and systems. They are 'Samatva' in its different connotations, 'Ahimsa', 'decentralization', 'samanvaya', 'satyagraha' and the principle of 'world peace'.

Samatva

Samatva is the very essence of Sarvodaya ideology. The term 'samatva' here, has been used in a very wider sense. It stands for unity, equality, equity, equanimity, balance and harmony in different perspectives and hence can be used in metaphysical, psychological, social, economic and political senses taken together. The Sarvodaya philosophy believes in oneness of the ultimate reality – that is God, Truth or Absolute. All beings of the universe are the manifestations of that one. Gandhi believes in the Upanishadic philosophy of- whatever is in the world, manifest or unmanifest, they are abode of God. In modern terminology, he used 'Truth' for 'God'. Nothing in the universe is devoid of truth. For Vinoba the Absolute is true and this world is its vibrant realty and human life is meant to realise the truth.[7] Thus, both Gandhi and Vinoba are monist and they regard life and the universe as Unity. This principle of unity is the foundation of all equalities. All people are metaphysically one and the same.

In society, Sarvodaya does not find any dichotomy between individual and society. What is good for the individual is good for society also. If non-violence is good for the individual it is also good for the society. For the interests of the society and individuals are the same. Gandhi envisaged good of the individual in the good of the society. Thus, in Sarvodaya, the principles of individual, family, nation and world communities are the same. As a natural corollary it follows that in society, no one is high or low by birth. Both Gandhi and Vinoba made a crusade against the exploitations of women, Harijan, Tribals, labourers and peasants in Indian society and racial discriminations in the other part of the world, which were against the principle of equality. They left no stones unturned to bring communal harmony in society. For them all religions are the different ways of reaching the same truth. According to Vinoba the different religions are the symbols of different values and every value is the sign of divinity. Thus all religions are ultimately one.

Sarvodaya economy is based on the principle of equality and it prescribes equal wages to a physical labourer and professionals like lawyers, doctors and teachers, for they have equal right to their livelihood. It is based on the principle of 'To each according to his need and from each according to his capacity'.[8] In order to bring equal economic opportunity, to all it glorifies economy based on bread- labour, Khadi and decentralised small scale industries, supplemented by the idea of trusteeship – a voluntary surrender of properties in the service of society.

To achieve the equanimity of mind and generate feeling of oneness of souls, sarvodaya philosophy adopts Gita's "Anashakti Yoga" or "Samya Yoga". A detached mind-free from worldly allurements and emotional disturbances, alone can enjoy the steadfastness of wisdom and live in the soul with full equanimity of mind. Vinoba in his "Samya sutrani" clearly writes that the goal of human life is to realize the highest equanimity (Avidheyam Param samyam) which can be possible by gradually realizing the smaller social, economic and psychological equalities in real life. He is not in favour of realizing this equanimity through artificial method of yoga.

Non-Violence (Ahimsa)

The next cardinal principle of Sarvodaya is non-violence. In Gandhi's philosophy "Truth is God" and Vinoba's message to humankind is to realize truth, throughout in one's life. It is clear that many faceted truth realization is the aim of Sarvodaya. Sarvodaya is the greatest truth from the social point of view. The only means to realize all forms of truth is non-violence, because there is a close relation between means and end. A right end cannot be achieved through bad means. Non-violence is a suitable means to realize the truth. The Marxian ideology compromises with the means but in Sarvodaya there is no compromise. As truth is many faceted, non-violence can not be one sided and restricted to individual's action in his personal life. Therefore, it is Sarvodaya ideology only, where we talk of non-violent society, economy, politics, education, world order, mass action, resistance etc. Principle of non-violence applies every where. If we do not apply this principle, we cannot raise the people above from-what Paulo Freire calls "The culture of silence".[9] Where, there is violence, there is fear, suppression, dominance and exploitation in various forms and vice-versa. In such a milieu Sarvodaya will be like sky-flower, not a reality.

Decentralization

Capitalism and socialism both follow the principle of centralization in the field of production. Sarvodaya on the contrary, believes in the principle of decentralization in its fullness. The idea of welfare to all logically implies the idea of 'welfare through all'. If the welfare programme is activised by one or a few, it will lead to the culture of domination. Similary, if production or wealth is concentrated in the hands of a few, in a limited area, that will never bring sarvodaya. In economics, centralization means, 'mass and centralized production'. In power politics, it is centralization of powers in one, in the case of monarchy and in a few, in the case of oligarchy. In individual life, centralization means accumulation of wealth and privileges due to excessive attachment for worldly upliftment. In other words, all sorts of possession (Parigraha) are also the forms of centralization.[10] In all these cases disparities among people increases and they give birth to violence, conflicts and war. Moreover, wealth, power and position-centralized in a few will be retained only by force and in such a situation, the concept of non-violent or sarvodaya society cannot be realized. It is, because of this, Gandhi said, "I hate privilege and monopoly what ever can not be shared by masses, is tabbo to me".[11] He believes that all kinds of centralization "cannot be sustained without adequate force" [12] and hence is inconsistent with the non-violent structure of society. His ideas of non-possession, village democracy, khadi and cottage industry-all are nothing but the application of the principle of decentralization which later on Vinoba and J.P. followed in toto.

Principle of Samanvaya or Synthesis

Metaphysically all living beings are one but empirically they belong to different cultures and society. From social point of view, each one grows and evolves towards perfection, through interaction with others. Therefore, sarvodaya does not find any conflict between diverging ideas, views, philosophies and cultures. It believes in the principle of samanvaya – that is proper acceptance of all. Samanvaya is not only a principle of synthesising different ideas and ideologies, but it is also a good method of adjustment and bringing harmony in society. The Indian philosophers basically believe in synthesis. Vedant,

Jainism and Buddhism – all believe in the principle of synthesis. Sarvodaya thinkers receive this idea from the legacy of Indian tradition. They tried to make different types of synthesis in their ideology. On the one hand they synthesized different noble ideas of the East and the West, on the other they synthesized theory with the practice; knowledge with action, education with life and man with nature. Though, Gandhi believed in indigenous principle, still he did not want to close the doors of other culture, rather wanted to keep them open so that air of different cultures may enter the room. Vinoba's synthesis of all religions in one of his prayers, is of par excellence.[13] He synthesised Gita, Vedant, Buddhism and Jainism with modern concept of the universe. J.P. Synthesised Gandhism and Marxism. Kaka sahib kalelkar was the ardent supporter of "samanvaya sanskriti" – synthetic cultures. Thus, principle of synthesis is the hard core of sarvodaya ideology. Without synthesis, culture of sarvodaya cannot develop. It may fall into dogma and inertia and lose its vitality.

Satyagraha

Sarvodaya, as a method of change, believes in the principle of Satyagraha. Satyagraha – positive or negative constructive or resistive, associative or dissociative – is the principle which can explain the resistance of evil while assisting the evil doers. It demands to act according to the judgement of one's conscience without any ill-will to the opponents. This may cause him confiscation of his property, physical affliction and even his death. A Satyagrahi believes in voluntary self-suffering and does not allow others to suffer for his ideas and truth. In other words, the principle of satyagraha is to act with one's soul-force which is generated by moral force or the force of love. The sarvodaya thinkers believe in the essential goodness of man and his change of heart through love and sacrifice. A permanent change in individual or society cannot take place with the use of physical power. The repressive method of physical powers – can result in the defeat of some one and the victory of others and they cannot promote sarvodaya. In the chain of violence and counter-violence, a conflicting situation may arise, in which welfare of all is impossible, as it demands a peaceful environment. It is the principle of satyagraha alone which can deliver good equally to the good as well as bad. It can fulfill the just demand without any harm and soften the cruel heart of the opponents. So both the parties are benefited. The constructive satyagraha can emancipate down trodden people, directly and create a strong people's power in society without harming the others.

Thus, both resistive and constructive Satyagraha are inevitable for the welfare of all. Gandhi applied this principle from his domestic life to international politics. Vinoba, during freedom struggle of India practiced both resistive and constructive satyagraha, but after independence, he devoted himself in realizing constructive satyagraha alone, in the form of Bhoodan-gramdan movement. J.P. maintained Gandhi's position throughout his life in practicing both resistive and constructive satyagraha which culminated in his movement of total revolution.

Principle of Peace

Peace is the highest principle of sarvodaya ideology. In fact other principles are various means for attaining peace in different aspects of our life. For sarvodaya thinkers peace is both a means to be adopted in solving different problems as well as an end to be sought to achieve in life. In their view, only peaceful methods are morally acceptable and all systems – political, social, economic and educational are desirable only when they promote peace in the individual and society. They use the term 'peace' in a wider sense. It stands both for 'the peace of mind and soul' on the one hand and 'peace of society and nations' on the other. In both the cases, 'peace' stands for happiness – either happiness of mind or soul or happiness of material pleasure in individual and social life.[14] Thus 'welfare to all' means 'peace of all kinds to all'. It encompasses in itself peace to all nations, i.e. world peace. Sarvodaya, devoid of peace, is a self-contradictory term. Though, the ultimate goal of sarvodaya is to realize spiritual peace which accrues from the highest equanimity, nevertheless, it does not undermine the value of material and partial peace in human life. It is true that the spiritual peace is complete and eternal and the material peace partial and temporal, yet the eternal cannot be achieved by a leap. It can be achieved gradually by realizing peace in day-today's life. Like the ascetics, sarvodaya thinkers do not reject the effort of worldly peace in the hope of the spiritual, rather they seek spiritual peace through the material and social peace of life.

According to Gandhi, ultimate happiness lies in the peace of individual and society. He wanted to use the weapon of non-violence "to abolish all wars, destroy all conflicts and settle all tensions".[15] He was of the firm view that a peaceful individual village, nation, alone can bring world peace.[16] He not only desired peace between Britain and India but "between warring nations of the earth".[17] As a matter of fact, he was the apostle of peace. Through out his life, he lived on the principle of peace and preached the gospel of peace in the hope that it must be realized, one day, in the whole of the individuals, nations and the world. It is needless to mention here Vinoba's concept of different equanimities to bring peace in life. He launched a peaceful revolution of Bhoodan-gramdan movement to settle land and social problems in India. His slogan 'let the world be happy' (Jai Jagat) is the symbol of his faith in world-peace. J.P. upto his last breathing strove hard to bring socio-economic and political peace in the world.

Thus, from the above discussion, we may conclude tentatively that Sarvodaya is a universal philosophy, based primarily on the six principles of equanimity, non-violence, decentralization, synthesis, satyagraha and world peace to be applicable in different facets of life and human creations. Our task is to explore its dimension on the basis of these principles as much as we can.

References and Notes

1. Sarvant vattad gun mukhya kalpanam,
sarvant sunyam cha mithonapekchham/
sarva pada manta kāram Nirantam,
sarvodayam tirthmidam tavaiva//

2. Arunchalam, k.: Gandhian Approach to Rural Development (Madurai; Sarvodaya illakkiya Pannai, 1981) p. 82.

3. Freire, Paulo; Pedagogy of the oppressed (U.K., Australia & Newzealand: Penguin Publication, Education Special series, 1970) p. 41.

4. Rao, V.K.R.V.: The Gandhian Alternative to western socialism (Bombay; Bhartiya Vidya Bhawan Publication) p. 47 & Arunachalam, K. ; 1981, pp. 85-86.

"Sarvodaya, the welfare of all, is a classless society based on the destruction of the classes but not on the destruction of the individuals who constitute the classes, a system of production that does not fail to make use of science and technology for creating an economy of abundance but does not in the process either kill individual initiative or freedom for development or create a psychology of ceaseless striving for more and more material goods, a system of distribution that will ensure a reasonable minimum income for all and while not aiming at a universal equality of an arithmetical kind, will never the less ensure that all private property or talent beyond the minimum will be used as a trust for the public good and not for individual aggrandisement, a social order where all will work but there is no inequality, either in status or in opportunity for any individual and a political system where change is the result of persuasion, differences are resolved by discussion and conflict by love and recognition of mutuality of interest and a life spent in dedication to God and cultivation of the spirit."

5. Varma, V.P.; The political philosophy of Mahatma Gandhi and Sarvodaya (Agra; Laxmi Narain Agrawal, 1980-81) 4th edn p. 280.

6. "The philosophy of Sarvodaya is based on the mystical intuitions and the social and political experiences of Gandhi. In his long life Gandhi attempted the synthesis of the ideas of Vedant, Buddhism, Tulsidas, Christianity, Ruskin, Talstoy, Thorean etc. ..... If Gandhism was merely a synthesis of moral intuitions and experiences, the sarvodaya philosophy tries to build a synthesis also of theoretical abstraction and political and economic generalizations" – Ibid. p. 280.

7. "Brahma Satyam, Jaganasfurtih,
Jivanam satya shodhanam." – Vinoba.

8. Note: - Vinoba adopts this theory on the logic of family institution (Parivarnyaya). In a family, there remain members of different categories like infant, child, grown up, old, male, female, healthy, sick, lazy, smart etc. Some earn more and some less but all incomes go to the family and all are benefited from it according to their need. Similarly, in society, people are of different capacities, so far their earning is concerned. But their basic needs can not be neglected in fulfillment as we do not neglect a child or an old or a sick person on the ground of their earnings.

9. Freire, Paulo; Cultural Action for Freedom (U.K. Newzealand Australia; Penguin Publication, Education Specials, 1974) p. 30.

10. Note: - I have used the term decentralization in a wide sense and included in it Aparigraha also, as it is nothing more than a principle of decentralization to be adopted in real life.

11. Tendulkar, D.G.; Mahatma (Bombay: Vithalbhai Jhaveri and D.G. Tendulkar, 1953) vol. 3, pp. 166-170.

12. Unnithan, T.K.N.; Gandhi and Social Change (Jaipur; Rawat Publication, 1979) p. 106.

13. "Aum tat sat sri narain tun
purushottam guru tun.
Siddha Buddha tun,
skand vinayaka savita pavak tun.
Brahma majda tun,
Yahava sakti tun,
Ishu pita prabhu tun
vashudeo go vishwarup tun
chidananda hari tun.
Adwitiya tun akal nirvaya
Atmalinga shiva tun."

In the above prayer, he synthesises all living religions like Adwaitism, Vaishnawism, Sikkhism, Jainism, Buddhism, Persian religion, Judaism, Christianity and Shaivism. He holds that the one and the same Absolute which is unique, eternal, fearless of the nature of Truth, consciousness and happiness is manifested in the dities of the above religions.

14. Acharyashri Tulsi, the head of the Terapanth sect(Jainism) has defined peace as:- "Peace is the name applied to that happiness, contentment or gladness whereby there is a peinliar vibration in the soul or awakening there of leading to consciousness about the real character of the soul. In worldly terminology, peace is also the name applied to that temporary mental or bodily happiness which results from the acquisition of some desired material object." – A Message of peace to a world full of unrest (Culcutta; Sri Jain Swetamber Terapanth sabha 1955) 2nd edn, p. 11.

15. Unnithan, T.K.N.; Gandhi and social change, opchit p. 112.

16. Ibid, p. 112.

17. Ibid, p. 112.

10

Mahatma Gandhi's Contribution to Indian Culture

Mahatma Gandhi – a sanatani Hindu, having deep faith in the fundamentals of Indian culture and profound impact of modern western thinkers like Tolstoy, Ruskin, Thureass and the ideas of the holi Bible expressed in the "**Sermon on the mount**" emboldened by the modern reformist movement of India initiated by Dr. Rajaram Mohan Roy and Dayanand Saraswati, with his rare original thinking and experience gathered from the experiment with Truth surrounded in life situation, contributed immensely to regenerate Indian Culture- both by reformist and revolutionary ideas and activities.

The culture of a nation gets expression through its body of knowledge, faith style of living and the institutions built for the realization of its cherished ideals and objects of life. Indian culture resides in Indian Philosophy, religion, ethics, art & literature, aesthetics as well as economic, political, social and educational institutions through which Indian people realize their goal of life. Mahatma Gandhi, by removing the inherent contradictions in Indian culture provided a fresh outlook in all the fields of Indian culture to live a better life here in this world and beyond.

Spiritual and moral consciousness are the chief characteristics of Indian Philosophy and religion. However, they are not free from contradictions. Philosophically Indian spirituality is grounded on one, pervasive and integral reality of Brahman or Absolute. But in practice classical concept of Indian spirituality is very narrow. It is individualistic passive, mystical, reclusive and to great extent life denying and otherworldly. Gandhi's concept of spirituality is distinctively a great improvement upon the classical concept. It is human, socialistic, activistic, rational and integral having both this worldly and transcendental upliftment, as we see in his concept of sarvodaya- welfare of all. The classical spirituality debars women from its practice and limits its practice only to male members of society. It is specially meant for the sages and those who are in the fourth stage of life i.e. Sanyasa. But for Gandhi spirituality is open to both male and female householders and sanyasin and youth and old. In fact, spirituality is the source of strength which helps us to fight all odds of life and hence relevant to all who live in this world. The most remarkable thing in Gandhi's spirituality is that it is not thing to be practiced in the forest or caves of the Himalayas, but to be realized through the real activities of life-social, economic, political and others.

The classical concept of spirituality aims at the realization of the infinite power of soul, infinite existence, consciousness and bliss. Gandhi's spirituality consists in identification with masses, especially poor, down trodden and deprived whom he called Daridranarayan and Harijan. Path of knowledge, devotion, meditation and selfless action are the paths of spiritual realization in classical spirituality. To Gandhi, selfless service of the people is the only way of self-realization which is called Moksha or Liberation. In the classical spirituality intuitive experience is the culmination of spirituality which is indescribable. Gandhi's spirituality is 'inner voice', 'soul-force', 'truth force', 'moral force' or 'the force of love', which is describable and practicable.

Gandhi's spiritual concept grew in the age of modern science. He realized the due importance of modern science. He was very much impressed by the humility, experimentation and exactitude of the modern science. Therefore he tried to synthesis science with his concept of spirituality in his thought as well action. Synthesis of truth with God, rationality with inner voice, body with soul in individual, physical treatment with Ramnam, material development with spiritual and moral development, individual freedom with social responsibility or Sarvodaya- are the fine examples of this synthesis. Thus, his metaphysics, epistemology, ethics, religion, education and socio-political and economic philosophies are based on the synthesis of science and spirituality. This synthesis enriched Indian culture and gave a new direction and vision to the people not only of Indian society but to the whole world.

The moral consciousness in Indian culture is also not free from its dichotomy. If reality is one and whole, how can one be moral in individual life and immoral in social behavior, pious in the place of worship and corrupt in office, moral in spiritual realization and immoral in mundane affair, pure in objective of life and impure in means to achieve it, conscious for transcendental morality and indifferent of social reality, good for individual and bad for society? Gandhi in his moral concept and life, tried to remove all these contradictions. To him, truth and non-violence are not to be practiced in personal life only, but also in social life, for what is good for the individual is also good for society and vice-versa. The good of individual is contained in the good of society is the first principle of Sarvodaya. Moral man and immoral society is inconceivable. Therefore Gandhi introduced Truth and Nonviolence in the concepts and activities of politics, economics, education and all social actions-constructive as well as resistive.

Similarly, Gandhi laid much stress on the purity of means along with the purity of end, specially in socio-political spheres. As truth and non-violence are relative terms and two facets of the same reality, so means and end are also relative terms and two facets of the same reality. In our life, we act in order to achieve some goal. When this goal is achieved, we proceed towards higher objective and this process goes on and on till we exist in this world. This makes it clear that reality is means in one context and end in another. If speaking truth in different fields of life is end, they must be actualized through non-violent means. To give a concrete shape to this principle, Gandhi adopted Satyagraha as means to achieve India's freedom, Swadeshi as means to curb foreign economic exploitation, non-co-operation and civil resistance as means to resist all the socio-political evils including economic disparities in society.

In ancient Indian philosophy, observance of five moral virtues i.e. Truth, Non-violence, Non-stealing, Celibacy and Non-possession are prescribed for the aspirant of personal salvation. Gandhi believed in mass salvation and for the aspirants of mass salvation whom he called Satyagrahi, prescribed to observe eleven vows including five of ancient ethics. Fearlessness, non satisfying of palate, bread-labour, equal treatment with all religions, swadeshi and touch ability – six other virtues were added by Mahatma Gandhi. Gandhi realized that observance of these six vows along with the ancient five is essential for a satyagrahi. Without fearlessness one cannot be truthful and non- violent and satyagrahi has to face many odd situations in course of his non-violent actions. So fearlessness is essential for those who are involved in social actions. Celibacy cannot be observed without observing 'aswad vrata'. Again social morality must be alive to the living situations of society.

Untouchability in Hindu society, foreign economic exploitation, communal disturbances and tendency to earn wealth without work, were the main problems in the realization of sarvodaya order of society in Gandhian era and most of them still exist in Indian society. To meet out these challenges, introduction of the four spatio-temporal morality was essential. If Gandhi were alive, he could have introduced two more vows-environmental protection and humanization of globalization. A culture cannot progress without enriching moral virtues from time to time according to the need of society. In this respect Gandhi's concept of mass salvation and addition of six other moral virtues are relevant and this should be regarded as very important contribution of Gandhi to Indian culture.

Like other cultures, Indian culture also believes in sin and merit (Pap and Punya) as the result of immoral and moral actions. However, these concepts are functional only. Charity and helping others are meritorious action and to inflict sufferings on others are sin. Gandhi's concept of merit and sin are mostly societal and structural. Politics without principle, wealth without work, pleasure without conscience, knowledge without character, commerce without morality, science without humanity and worship without sacrifice-are seven social sin, mostly structural than functional and more fundamental. This is new dimension of merit and sin in Indian ethics and very important contribution in moral consciousness.

Unlike western utilitarianism of greatest good of the greatest number, Indian culture holds this world as a family and hence, believes in the welfare of all. Rig Veda's hymns, Ishavashyam idam sarwam of Ishavashyopanishad, "Sarvabhuthiteerthah" of the Gita, Buddha's "Bahujan hitaya bahujan sukhay", Jain's "Parasparopagraho Jivanam," and "Sarve bhawantu sukhinah" of Mahabharata- all are expressions of sarvodaya. However, the Sarvodaya expressed in ancient

Indian philosophy is in the form of pious feelings and goodwill, Gandhi developed the concept as a complete philosophy and also tried to reconstruct Indian society accordingly. Some of the important ideas, which he developed in sarvodaya philosophy are-

1. The good of the individual is contained in the good of society.
2. The Wages for intellectual worker as well as physical worker should be equal and equitable, for they all earn for their livelihood.
3. The work of manual workers is the best.
4. Grievances with others should be resolved by peaceful and non-violent means of Satyagraha, civil resistance and non-co-operation.
5. The real owner of physical, mental and material resources is God or society and hence one should use them as a trustee.
6. The socio-politico-economic structure of society should be such in which every member of society may realize his or her potentialities.
7. Development should be all round development and for all.
8. Education must be man-making education.
9. Selfless social service should be regarded as the path of self realization.

The above ideas are meant to develop a non-violent society and sarvodaya culture which should be regarded as special contribution of Mahatma Gandhi to Indian culture.

Truth and Reality are two well known concepts of philosophy- both eastern and western. In the theories of western philosophy truth is regarded as property of proposition, through which we get knowledge. A proposition may be true, if it corresponds to the reality. It may be true if it is consistent with previous propositions of the argument and it may be true if it works in life. Hegel goes to the extreme by saying, "Real is rational and rational is real" i.e. Truth belongs to rationality. In Indian philosophy the concept of truth is derived from the word 'Sat', which means 'existence'. The concept is also used in the sense of a property of speech and a 'moral way of life'.

Gandhi's concept of truth is most comprehensive and a development upon both propositional truth of the west and existential and moral truth of the east. In fact, his truth is integral constituting truth of metaphysics, epistemology, moral philosophy as well as truth of science and societal truth. He defined truth as "universal principle" – applicable in every field of life and consciousness. It is also not limited to the property of a speech but inclusive of all moral actions, thought and way of life. His is both relative and absolute truth. The absolute truth is God which is infinite existence, consciousness and bliss and also good and beautiful. Gandhi relates truth and God by his logic that law and law giver are one. Universal principle is the law and God is the law giver. A moral agent may proceed towards moral action either believing in universal laws or universal law' given the result will be the same.

According to Gandhi, truth is realized through practice and experiment in our life. It is known through inner voice after living a moral life possible for all, irrespective of the seers. But Gandhi is aware of the fact that one can realize only relative truth and progress from relative truth to other higher relative truth approaching the absolute truth. Gandhi believed that perfect truth and non-violence cannot be realized from this mortal frame of body, but in seeking relative truth, one can certainly achieve the nearness of absolute truth or God. It is worth to be noted here that in his first experience Gandhi realized that 'God is truth'. If we try to understand God through his attributes, truth alone is the most comprehensive and faultless attribute which can define God. Later on he realized the inadequacy of this proposition, as it will not be acceptable to the atheists and scientists, who don't believe in God. Again we find that the fanatics committed innumerable violence in the name of God. But truth is acceptable to both atheists and scientists and has moral background. Finding this universality of truth Gandhi identified God with absolute truth and said "Truth is God". Here Gandhi tried to synthesize science with religion and rationality with faith.

Gandhi accepts truth as a way of life in which one confesses and corrects one's evil and proceeds towards goodness, seeking more and more universal laws. This way of life needs commitment to live with truth. Gandhi also used the concept in the sense of force or energy. He called it "truth-force", equivalent to "moral-force", "soul-force" and "force of love". The person, who uses this force alone in life, is called satyaghahi. Gandhi applied this force in the freedom struggle of India and created a unique history in the world. As a way of life, Gandhi's truth is always growing and fresh. There is no staticism in it. The western mind fails to comprehend Gandhi's truth and seeks consistency in his statements criticizing it as a "meaningful flux." But this is wrong from the analysis above, it is most candid that Gandhi's truth is most comprehensive, rational, scientific and practical. It comprehends all the fields of our life and therefore, is a great development from the concepts of orient and occident.

Non-violence is the supreme concept in Indian morality- "Ahimsa Parmodharmah". However, this concept has not a definite meaning. In the Yogasutra of Patanjali, it is used in the sense of giving up of hatred – "Ahimsa Vaira Tyagraha". In the Prashnavyakaran Sutra of the Jain, it has sixty four synonyms.

Acharanga Sutra of the same religion uses the term in the sense of non-killing, non-injury, non-exploitation and non-domination. Non-violence in this religion covers up both inner or mental and outer or physical non-violence (Bhaav Ahimsa and dravya-ahimsa). Buddha used the term in the sense of compassion and amity. All the meanings show that in ancient Indian culture, the term was used only in the sense of personal morality both negatively and positively. Gandhi gave a new dimension to the concept. To him, Ahimsa is not only a kind of moral behaviour of a person; but also the characteristics of social structure. An economic, political, social, educational system and our style of living may be violent and non-violent. Ahimsa is as wide as truth, for both are the two sides of the same coin. If we want to define Gandhi's non-violence, the definition will be as such – 'that which helps to sustain life is non violence and that which obstructs the growth of life is violence'. This definition will be applicable to both personal and impersonal, direct and indirect, functional and structural non-violence. Modern peace scientists like Paulo Freire and John Galtung hold that Gandhi's importance lies in exploring structural violence pervaded in society. When Gandhi said – "Hate the evil, not evil doers", "Hate the capitalism not capitalists". He meant to advise to root out structural violence from society, which is more fundamental than the functional violence of evil doers. Exploitation, disparity in income and domination are structural violence for they are rooted in our social structure of which people are not conscious. People in general are responsible to maintain such exploitative structure which is cause of functional violence visible to us. To root out structural violence from society, we need organized effort on the part of the people. It is ironical that in India today, we raise our voice against tainted ministers but want to maintain the system intact, responsible for it. We want to have an egalitarian society but maintain rather strengthen the exploitative and dominating structure of economy as well as society which is responsible for mass poverty, disparities and exploitations. We want quick justice but maintain the judicial system responsible for the 'justice delayed and justice denied'. We want to root out corruption from bureaucracy but maintain complicated administrative system. We desire mass employment, but maintain educational system responsible for mass unemployment. Corruption, injustice, exploitation, unemployment, disparities and to force some people to live the life of poverty are greater violence than the violence of killing, torturing and hating. Gandhi in his concept of non-violence brought to our notice that structural non-violence is a precondition to a peaceful and sarvodaya society. This is a welcome addition not only in Indian culture but the culture of the whole world.

Gandhi's idea of trusteeship is an attempt to give non-violent solution to the problem of ownership and distribution of wealth. Basically it is a legal concept, but Gandhi owed it from the Hindu culture and applied it in socio-economic context. In the Rig Veda it is said that the earth is our mother and we are her sons. In Ishavashyopanishad, the first verse says – 'This world is the abode of God'. Whatever we have in this world, the real owner of it is God.

Hence, one is entitled to enjoy after offering things to God. Gandhi gave new meaning to ideas of earth and God. To him the ideas are symbol of 'society'. The real meaning is that whatever we have, its real owner is society and we are its trustee. It means an individual may have his private property but he will use it in the interest of society. One is entitled to receive only for his essential needs and the surplus wealth must be used for society. Not only wealth, but his intellect and labour also should be used for the benefit of society, not for his self-interest. The socialist theory "To each according to his need and from each according to his capacity" is acceptable to Gandhi provided it is managed voluntarily and freely.

The idea of trusteeship has been placed before Indian people as an alternative of capitalism and socialism. The capitalism believes in private ownership and freedom of production. But it promotes exploitation to the poor. Socialism believes in state ownership of resources but it kills the incentive for production. Therefore, Gandhi suggests, one be allowed to keep private property but he must use it in the interest of society. People question the practicability of this outlook. But Gandhi said, "If trusteeship will not do, non-co-operation will do."

Vinoba, the disciple of Gandhi, called the idea "Vishwasta Vritti" and he gave the idea practical shape in his Bhoodan-Gramdan movement. Here also we find that Gandhi's trusteeship is a development as social morality from the ancient idea of personal morality.

Gandhi's concept of man and civilization are the outcome of Indian philosophy and culture. In both the orthodox and heterodox traditions of Indian philosophy, except the Charvaks, man is considered as combination of body and soul. The Jain believe that man is the combination of pudgala and jiva (matter and soul). Lord Buddha apparently denied the existence of soul, yet held that man is nothing but the union of five Skandha and Chetnapravaha (matter and stream of consciousness). For the Sankhya- Yoga philosophy, man is the meeting ground of prakriti and purusha (matter and consciousness). Man in Advaita Vedanta is accidentally body, but essentially soul which is not different from Brahman. However, all the systems hold that the body aspect of man is temporal, accidental and instrumental. Therefore, the Summum Bonum of life is liberation of soul from the bondage of body, which is possible if material demands of man is controlled by Dharma or morality.

Gandhi on the line of Indian seers also held that man is both body and soul. Body is like a rented house in which we are to pay for its use. Soul is the real owner of body. Unfortunately, due to his ignorance, man identifies himself with body alone and his all efforts are directed to serve only body, neglecting moral conduct and soul consciousness, which is source of permanent peace and happiness. Due to attachment with the body, he becomes prey of immoral conduct which is source of all evils. With the help of moral actions, he overpowers his evils and gradually progress towards the realization of soul. Thus, according to Gandhi, man is the mixture of both good and evil.

Contrary to Indian tradition, for the western philosophers man is a psychological, biological and material being and to seek sensual pleasure is the goal of his life. Modern western civilization is erected on this presumption.

Gandhi warned the Indian people against the attraction of modern civilization, which is immoral, Godless and founded on wrong conception of man and his destiny. Matter has replaced spirituality in modern western civilization. No doubt, there are some good points in modern civilization but on the whole, it is worthless, self-defeating and contains in itself the seed of all crisis we face today. Gandhi opined that it is nine days wonder and will be crushed from its own weight. Hence, he advised Indian people to live in true civilization which is founded in Indian culture.

A true civilization, according to Gandhi, means good conduct. A good conduct is possible not in high standard of living but in a high standard of life and high standard of life consists in simple living and high thinking. Happiness doesn't consist in increasing our wants but in reducing it or wantlessness. For mind is a restless bird to which more you give, more it wants, says Gandhi. High sense of consumerism cannot give us stable peace and happiness.

In true civilization, there will be synthesis of science and spirituality. Science, in exploring physical laws, makes our existential life better. But it does not know what is good and what is bad. It is amoral. It cannot change our inner consciousness like greed, hatred, anger and infatuation. Spirituality alone can raise our moral life and provide lasting peace and happiness. Hence, in new civilization, science will follow the direction given by spirituality.

The modern western civilization believes in mass production and material prosperity. It requires high technology and large scale industries. On the contrary true civilization believes in production by the masses with the help of small scale industries and agriculture using small machines. It does not mean that high technology and big industries will be totally vanished. In new civilization state will run some big industries to produce instruments for structural changes with the help of heavy machines.

The development model of new civilization will be radically different from modern civilization. It will be neither capitalistic nor socialistic, which believes in material development only. In new civilization, development will be integral development of both man and society including moral and spiritual development.

The politics of new civilization will also go under change. The parliamentary democracy will be replaced by true democracy which Gandhi called 'Ramarajya'. In a true democracy, there will be no disparities among people. All will live a harmonious life, with mutual trust and love. The punishment policy will be changed into reforming policy with the help of non-violence. State power will be replaced by Lokaniti. There will be no discrimination between minority and majority. People will use non-violent technique for resolving all kinds of conflict including war. The idea of Ramarajya will be actualized through Gramarajya and Panchayatirajya.

Thus, Gandhi's concepts of man and civilization are refinement and enlargement of Indian culture. True civilization is founded on the true nature of man with the ideal of Sarvodaya. The ideas which were used in Indian culture for the personal life, Gandhi developed a complete structure of society from those moral and spiritual ideas.

In India, religion and politics were inseparably related to each other. Politics bereft of religion was condemned as it causes sufferings to the people. In the Shanti Parva and Anushashan Parva of Mahabharata a detailed description of dharma and adharma, i.e. what ought to do and what ought not to do, has been given. For people in general and ruler in particular, the Mahabharata gives a brief description of dharma as 'what conduct we disapprove in our personal life, should not be done to others'. Prashastpada defines dharma as 'that which promotes our worldly as well as transcendental life is dharma' (Yatoabhyudayasya nihshreyash siddhi, sa dharmah). In Jain philosophy dharma is taken as ten virtues. Buddhism and Manusmriti also describe dharma as ten virtues differently from the Jainas. Non-violence is regarded as supreme religion (Puramdharma) for both people and ruler. Thus, the concept of dharma in Indian culture has been used either in the sense of moral conduct or moral virtues. What is good is dharma and what is bad is adharma. Politics cannot be devoid of good conduct and hence, dharma is part and parcel of politics.

Aristotle in western philosophy also accepted ethics as the subject of politics. If the idea of good is the main concern of ethics, how can politics be devoid of ethics which is concerned to deliver good to the people?

Mahatma Gandhi in modern India, emphatically said, "Politics of religion is a death trap". However, the religious politics of Mahatma Gandhi is misconceived today by those who hold themselves as champion of secularism. To remove this misunderstanding it is pertinent to clarify Gandhi's concept of dharma, different from the western concept of religion. Gandhi used the concept of dharma in four senses – in the sense of truthful and non-violent conduct, organized religions, personal faith and spirituality. All the meanings show that Gandhi's dharma is also not opposed to secularism which condemns theism and glorifies materialism, humanism, science and rationality and moral upliftment.

When Gandhi said, 'politics cannot be separated from religion', he meant to say that politicians must obey the rules of truth and non-violence, for what is good in personal life, is also good in political life. This led Gandhi to open politics based on satyagraha and non-violent actions and condemn garbed diplomacy based on untruth and violence. He also gave a picture of non-violent state. Gandhi believed that violence and democracy go ill together. Politics which is a managerial concept, should not be done by the criminals and corrupt.

Gandhi's use of 'religion' in second and third sense is also essential for democratic state and government. A democratic state government must pay equal respect to all religions and faiths. The politicians should not favour or disfavour a particular religion. They should give equal treatment to all faiths irrespective of minority and majority, to obey rule of law and democracy. Communal harmony, protection of diversity and equal respect to all the sects of the country are the moral imperative of today and tomorrow. When Gandhi used 'religion' in the sense of 'spirituality' he meant to glorify the spirit of selfless service with religious purity and commitment in politics.

To observe truth and non-violence, to give equal respect to all religions and to do selfless social service, with a programme of constructive work for the villagers, are essentially moral concepts. Therefore, Gandhi's concept of religion is essentially ethical as he said 'ethical religion' and 'religious ethics' are identical.

Gandhi's concept of religious politics is not opposed to the secular politics of the West. When we talk of the secular politics, we mean that state has nothing to do with the religious matter. It has to perform material and social work to promote socio-economic conditions of the people. This is why in the twilight of his life he said that state has nothing to do with religion. It should perform mundane work, like improvement of economic and social conditions of people, currency and other structural works. Thus we find that state and government may be religious and secular at the same time for even material and social progress are not possible without observing the rules of morality. Unfortunately in modern Indian politics neither of the parties observe rules of religion and secularism and hence, both are in danger. Politics has concern neither with moral conduct nor with social and material progress. They use the term secular only for the purpose of vote bank. Pro-Hindu is called communal and pro-muslim secular. In fact both are communal and none of them is secular. Ethical religion is far from the politicians. If India has to progress, there must be marriage of religion and politics in Gandhian sense.

Thus , the 'Rajadharma' of Hindu culture is amply clarified and extended particularly in modern conditions of India, in the thought and action of Mahatma Gandhi. I think this is very much relevant for the modern politicians groping in the darkness of power politics.

Gandhi's contribution in social reform of India is also remarkable. He believed in the Varnasharam Vyavastha of Hindu society, which to him, is scientific, natural and has capacity to solve the world problem of unemployment. But nowhere in India Varnasharam Vyavastha exists today. It has degenerated into caste system. Caste system in itself is not bad. According to Gandhi, as it is natural than the class system of the West. People inherit the profession of their ancestors and learn them in natural way. They don't wander for their employment in this system. But the two evils of the caste system- untouchability and casteism are intolerable for Gandhi which are eating into the vitality of Hindu society. He took the challenge of removal of untouchability and casteism. He edited Harijan to highlight the problems of scheduled castes, who were deprived of their human rights by the casteist Hindus. He included removal of untouchability in his constructive programmes as well as eleven vows of satyagrahi. He also suggested interdining and intercaste marriage to weaken these practices. By Gandhi's effort untouchability in Hindu society and apartheid in the West has become non-entity in educated society. However, casteism is strengthened day by day due to dirty politics, which Indian people have to take as a challenge.

Gandhi was the champion of social justice in modern India. In Hindu society discrimination is made between untouchables and caste, evaluation of manual work and intellectual work and male and female. Gandhi raised his voice against all this discrimination. To him, all castes, works and sexes are equal, for they serve the same purpose of society and hence, have same moral value. None is high and none is low.

Women in India, though are in high esteem theoretically, but practically they are subordinated by men and have been debarred from many rights which men enjoy. To Gandhi women are co-ordinate of men, equal partner in the ventures of life. Metaphysically both men and women are same, as they are essentially soul. They are equal in their abilities. However, male partner due to gender bias have created several disabilities in women. Women have been made subject of enjoyment. Gandhi said that women should enjoy all the rights which men enjoy. He engaged them in national freedom movement of India and pleaded for their participation in social work. He pleaded for their education and full growth of their personality like men. For the empowerment of women, he condemned child marriage, purdah system and deodasi system, which were the main hurdles in the empowerment of women and their education. Due to Gandhi's efforts, today women are doing excellent jobs in all fields of life. Women's emancipation is an important contribution of Gandhi to Indian society.

To conclude, synthesis of science and spirituality, compreshensive meanings and extensive experiment on truth and non-violence, picture of a true civilization on the true foundation of human nature, synthesis of religion, spirituality and morality with secularism in politics and social justice to weaker sections of people in Indian society are the main contribution of Gandhi to Indian culture.

Glossary

1.	Absolute	God.
2.	Adam Smith	A Scottish economist.
3.	Ahimsa	Non violence.
4.	Ahimsa Parmo dharma	A sanskrit phrase used in Hindu Dharmah mythological texts viz Mahabharat, Bhagavat Geeta etc., meaning thereby "Non-violence is the ultimate Religion."
5.	Ahimsa vaira	Concept in Jainism ; Tyagraha
6.	Arnold Toynbee	An eminent modern historian of West.
7.	AIDS	A desease.
8.	Athens	A town of Rome.
9.	Ashram	A place of abode and activity for disciplined community members.

10.	Aurobindo	An eminent Indian philosopher.
11.	Aristotle	An eminent Greek philosopher.
12.	Antonio Salazar	A Portugese politician and economist.
13.	Amartya Sen	An Indian economist.
14.	Arthashashtra	A treatise on Statecraft, economic policy and military strategy, written by Indian economist kautilya@chanakya
15.	Aldous Huxley	An English writer considered to be a leader of modern thought.
16.	Babylon	A famous city of ancient Greece.
17.	Belgium	A city of Germany.
18.	Bernard Crick	A British political theorist and democratical socialist.
19.	Brahman	Member of the first of the four castes in India, whose chief duty is the study of the Vedas and the performance of sacrifices and other religious rituals.
20.	B.R. Ambedkar	One of leading Indian freedom fighter and draftsman of Indian Constitution.

21.	Bertrend Russell	A British philosopher social reformist and pacifist.
22.	Britain	England.
23.	Buddha, Lord	The founder of Buddhism; in about 483 B.C.
24.	Bhudan-Gramdan	A social movement of distributing land and village among have-nots; Binoba started begging land from the land-lord and distributed it among the people who were landless.
25.	Bahujan Hitaya (Bahujan Sukhay)	Means welfare and happiness for large numbers (the good of masses, the benefit of masses).
26.	Bhava Ahimsa	Inner or mental non-violence.
27.	Constantinople	A town and capital of ancient Roman Empire.
28.	Cancer	A disease.
29.	Christ	Name of Christian God.
30.	Clemont	A western truth mystic.
31.	Christian	A religious sect (group).
32.	Chipko Movement	A movement started by Sundar Bahuguna in Indian Himalayan range to preserve the forests.

33.	Canada	A country of North America.
34.	Charvak	An ancient Indian philosopher.
35.	Caste system	In Indian society the people were divided into several groups according to their work.
36.	Czech	Of Czechoslovakia.
37.	Comenius	An eminent Czech educator in 1592-1670.
38.	Diabetics	A disease.
39.	Dominique Pire	A Belgian clergyman and educator, awarded Noble prize for peace in 1958.
40.	Dutch	People of Holland.
41.	Dayanand Saraswati	Swami Dayanand Saraswati (1824-1883), founder of the Arya Samaj in India.
42.	Daridranarain	God in the form of the poor and the destitute.
43.	Dravya Ahimsa	Physical Non- violence.
44.	Erik H. Erikson	Danish German American pshychoanalyst.
45.	Emerson	American philosopher.
46.	Europe	A continent
47.	England	A country of Europe.
48.	E.F. Schumacher	British economist.
49.	France	A country of Europe.
50.	Froebel	German educationist.

51.	Gandhi Mahatma	Father of Nation of India, who led the freedom movement (struggle) of India in 20th century against Britain: also a great philosopher.
52.	Gandhism	The philosophy established by Gandhi.
53.	Gerald Heard	A British historian, educator and philosopher.
54.	Ramchandran	An Indian philosopher.
55.	Gandhian	Follower of Gandhi.
56.	Ganga	A pious river of North India.
57.	Gokhale	A strong leader of freedom movement of India and the political teacher of Gandhi
58.	Germany West	A country of Europe.
59.	Gita	A Hindu scriptural work in sanskrit verse, composed some centuries before the christian era, in which Sri Krishna sums up the essence of Hindu religion and philosophy.
60.	Gurukul	The schools of ancient India which were situated in a peaceful place near forests and the rivers, where the students lived a simple life.

61.	Gujarati	People of Gujarat, a state of India.
62.	Gramrajya	Government of the village.
63.	Hind Swaraj	A magazine of India published during freedom struggle.
64.	Herbert Muller	An American historian and academician.
65.	Harijan	A magazine by Gandhi.
66.	Himsa	Violence.
67.	Harishchandra	An eminent king of ancient India who never told a lie and reigned with full justice and love.
68.	Hebrews	The Jews.
69.	Harijan Basti	The living place of the minial caste among Hindus.
70.	Himalayan Blunder	Its a proverb, meaning a great, as great as the mountain Himalayas.
71.	Hindu	Ancient Indian religion.
72.	Hinduism	Attribute of Hindus.
73.	Himalaya	A range of mountain situated in north of India.
74.	Hegel	A German philosopher.
75.	Italy	A country of Europe.
76.	Indian Home Rule	A magazine Published during freedom struggle of India.

77.	Imam Hassan	family member of Md. Paigamber (founder of Islam)
78.	Imam Hussain	Do.
79.	Iraq	A country of South-west Asia.
80.	India	A country of Asia.
81.	Isavashyo- Panishada	One of the major Upanishadas, an old Hindu scripture).
82.	Jerusalem	A town of Israel.
83.	Judaism	A set of beliefs and practices originating in the Hebrew Bible and is considered to be one of first Monotheistic religion.
84.	John Robinson	English Writer.
85.	John Galtury	Philosopher of modern America.
86.	Jew	A member of the Hebrew race
87.	Jay Prakash	A freedom fighter of India and a socialist.
88.	Julian Huxley	An English evolutionary biologist, humanist and interventionists.
89.	John Dewey	An American philosopher, psychologist and educational reformer.
90.	Japan	A famous small country of north-east Asia.
91.	Joint family	A family where all the member of family, i.e.; father, mother, brother,

		sister; all live together under one administration.
92.	Jainism	An Indian religion.
93.	Khadi	Cloth spinned by handloom.
94.	K. D. Gangrade	An Indian Gandhian philosopher.
95.	Khuda	God (Urdu word).
96.	Kenneth slowe	A British administrator.
97.	Kautilya	An eminent economist and politician of ancient India.
98.	Kshatriya	Member of the second of the four castes of Hindus, whose chief duty is to fight, to reign and to protect the people.
99.	K. Arunachalam	Indian economist.
100.	Kaka Saheb Kaleker	A Gandhian thinker.
101.	Lokaniti	Law for the people.
102.	Loksewaka	Person who live in the service of the people.
103.	London	Capital of U.K.
104.	Lennard Vriens	A peace educationists from Holland.
105.	Moksha	Salvation, liberation from earthly bondage.
106.	Maharshi Aurobindo	A great Indian philosopher.
107.	Mohammad	Muslim prophet.
108.	Mahatma	Great soul, title given to Gandhiji by Rabindra Nath Tagore.

109.	Mohandas Karamchand Gandhi	Mahatma Gandhi's real name.
110.	Mammon	God of wealth that is Kuber.
111.	Mussalman	Mohammedon (follower of Islam).
112.	Martin Luther King Junior	An American thinker and social reformer
113.	Montessory Lady	An eminent educationists; a form of Infant education that was named after this lady.
114.	Mahavir Lord	24th Tirthankar or Prophet of Jainism (about 468 B.C.) who is popularly regarded as its greatest promulgator, originally named Vardhamana.
115.	Mahabharata	Hindu epic having the theme of the story of war between Pandwas and Kourwas, cousins and princes of the Lunar race for throne of Hastinapur (ancient Delhi).
116.	Manusmriti	An ancient hindu book of social and moral ethics written by the sage Manu.
117.	New Delhi	Capital of India.

118.	Naomi Wolf	An American author and political consultant.
119.	Nehrurian	Follower of Pandit Jawahar Lal Nehru, the first Prime Minister of India.
120.	National Congress	The political party that struggled for the freedom of India.
121.	Netherlands	A country in north-west Europe.
122.	Non-Co-operation	The act of non co-operating with the established Government.
123.	Narmada Valley Protection Movement	A movement started by Medha Patil to protect the river Narmada of India.
124.	Nirvana	Salvation.
125.	Oestreich	A German educator.
126.	Paris	Capital of France.
127.	Pandit Jawaharlal Nehru	First Prime Minister of India after having independence.
128.	Pyarelal	Private secretary to Mahatma Gandhi.
129.	Prahalad	Son of the demon Hirnayakashyap, who became the devotee of Lord Vishnu and always got protection from Lord Vishnu against his father's prosecution.

130.	Paulo Freire	A pedagogue and educationists of modern world in America.
131.	Pakistan	A country of Asia.
132.	Parsi	People of the country Pharas that is now Iran, member of Zoroastrian community.
133.	Pestalozzi	An educationist born in Zurich. A swiss pedagogue and educational reformer.
134.	Parasparo Pagraho	Means Interdependence. A concept from Jainism denoting that "all life is bound together by mutual support and interdependence".
135.	Patnjali	Known as 'Father of Yoga' born in India, an ancient physician.
136.	Panchayat rajya	Rule of the Panchayata, a council of five.
137.	Rome	Capital of Italy.
138.	Radhakamal Mukherjee	An Indian thinker and social scientist of modern India.
139.	Ramchandra	Hero of the great Hindu epic 'Ramayana'.
140.	Rene Dubos	French-American, Author of maxim 'Think globally, act locally'.
141.	R.P. Mishra	An Indian philosopher.

142.	Ramayana	Hindu epic
143.	Rama	The Hero of Hindu epic Ramayana.
144.	Rasool	A muslim prophet.
145.	Rajdharma	Religion of state; Hindu code of religious and moral duty of a state.
146.	Robert Sperlogh	A peace educationist.
147.	Roussea	A Swiss philosopher.
148.	Ruskin	A British critic and social thinker.
149.	Raja Ram Mohan Roy	A social reformer of India who abolished the 'Sati-pratha' in which wife was burnt alive with her dead husband.
150.	Rigveda	Vedas are most ancient Hindu scriptures composed of hymns to various deities.
151.	Ramrajaya	administration based on religious and moral duties.
152.	Sat	Truth; a sanskrit word has three meanings 1. That which is changeless 2. That which exists 3. That which is good.
153.	Sabhyata	Civilization
154.	Sanskriti	Culture
155.	Shepard B. Clough	An American economist.
156.	Spain	A country of western Europe.

157.	Sweden	A country of north-west Europe.
158.	Swaraj	Self-administration, administration by own people.
159.	Sachchidananda	Name of God in Hinduism, the God whose abode is truth.
160.	Satyam, Shivam, Sundaram	Truth; Goodness and Beauty.
161.	Switzerland	A country of middle Europe.
162.	South Africa	A country in remote south of Africa
163.	Swadesh	Of one's own country.
164.	Swadeshi	Related to one's own country.
165.	Satyagrahi	The person who resort on satyagraha.
166.	Swami Vivekanand	An Indian eminent religious philosopher.
167.	Satyagraha	Recourse to truth-force or soul-force.
168.	Swadharma	Religion of self.
169.	Sarvodaya Movement	That great movement in which everybody will live, will rise and will be happy.
170.	Shanti Sainik	One who fights without arms
171.	Shanti mantras	Sacred chants for peace.
172.	Sudra	Member of the fourth caste among Hindus treated as menial caste.

173.	Sarvodaya	Progress and development of all, of everybody.
174.	Acharya Samanta Bhadra	A Jain philosopher.
175.	Sankhaya Yoga	Twin system of Indian philosophy.
176.	Shankracharya	Hindu philosopher of the 8th century A.D., who was one of the fore most exponents of Non-dualism of the Vedanta school of philosophy.
177.	Shanti Parwa	A chapter of Hindu Epic 'Mahabharat'
178.	Sanyasa	Abandonment of all worldly ties to concentrate on the Supreme being.
179.	Sarvabhuta Teerthah	It bars violence against "all creatures" *(sarva-bhuta)* except at the "holy places" *(tirtha)* where ritual sacrifice was performed.
180.	Sarve buawantu Sukhinah	A prayer wishing happiness for all.
181.	Shashtras	The Hindu scriptures.
182.	T.B.	A disease 'Tuberculosis'.
183.	Toynbee	An eminent modern historian.
184.	Ted Robert Gurr	An American political thinker and writer.
185.	Tolstoy	A Russian Author and philosopher.

186.	U.S.A	United Kingdom of America.
187.	U.N.D.P. Policy	United Nations Development Program
188.	United Nations Organisation	A group of nations formed after second world war.
189.	Utrecht	A toon and Province in the Netherlands.
190.	Upanishad	Ancient Hindu philosophical Treatises, appended to the Vedas and regarded as equally authoritative as the Vedas.
191.	Upanishadak	Related to Upanishad.
192.	Verrier Elvin	A self-trained anthropologist and tribal activist, who began his career in India as a missionary
193.	Vinoba	A saint philosopher of India in twentieth century.
194.	Varnashram	Four fold divisions of Hindu society. Arrangement of the Hindu society on four fold divisions based on hereditary occupations.
195.	Varna	Four divisions of Hindu society i.e. Brahman, Kshtriya, Vaishya and Shudra.

196.	Vasudhaiva Kutumbakum	The whole world is a family
197.	Vishnu	Hindu name of God 'the Foster'.
198.	Vishesh Dharma	That moral and religious duty which should be performed suddenly at a special occasion.
199.	Vaisya	Member of the third caste among Hindu.
200.	Village Panchayat	A body of five person in village to administer the village.
201.	Vedantik	Related to Vedas the most ancient Hindu scriptures, composed of hymns for various deities.
202.	Vishwasta Vrite	To live with the trust on others.
203.	V.K.R.V. Rao	An Indian economist and educationist.
204.	V.P. Verma, Prof.	Ex-professor of Political Science in Patna University, Bihar, India.
205.	Vedant	A system of philosophy springing from the upnishads.
206.	Wallace	A British naturalist, explorer, geographer, anthropologist and biologist.
207.	Walter Hilton	A western truth mystic.

208.	Washington	A famous toon of U.S.A.
209.	World League	An organisation of nations.
210.	Yogasutra	The rules of Hindu system of contemplation for effecting union of the human soul with the Supreme Being.

Index